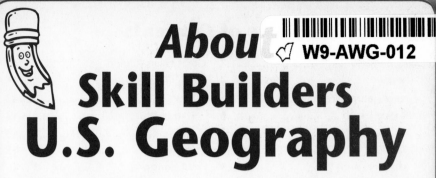

About
Skill Builders
U.S. Geography

by Isabelle McCoy and Leland Graham

Welcome to Rainbow Bridge Publishing's Skill Builders series. Like our Summer Bridge Activities collection, the Skill Builders series is designed to make learning both fun and rewarding.

Skill Builders U.S. Geography helps students reinforce their knowledge of U.S. states. Each Skill Builders volume is grade-level appropriate, with clear examples and instructions to guide the lesson. U.S. Geography includes readings, exercises, and activities on regions, state facts, history, topographical features, population, and more.

Learning is more effective when approached with an element of fun and enthusiasm—just as most children approach life. That's why the Skill Builders combine entertaining and academically sound exercises with eye-catching graphics and fun themes—to make reviewing basic skills at school or home fun and effective, for both you and your budding scholars.

Table of Contents

New England Region

The New England region includes Maine, Rhode Island, Vermont, New Hampshire, Connecticut, and Massachusetts. The Appalachian Mountains separate the New England region from the states to the west. The Appalachians in this region include the Green Mountains and the White Mountains. These mountains are sources of marble and granite. The highest peak in the region is Mount Washington, which is 6,288 feet (1,917 m) tall. The windiest place on earth is on top of Mount Washington.

The northern end of the Appalachian Trail is found in Baxter State Park in Maine. This trail stretches along the eastern coast of the United States to Georgia.

The longest river in the New England region is the Connecticut River. It begins in northern New Hampshire and flows south along the New Hampshire-Vermont border. This river flows across Massachusetts and Connecticut to Long Island Sound in New York.

Tourism is an important source of income year round because of the many historical sites located here. Manufacturing and forestry are also important to the region's economy. Electronic equipment, computer components, airplane parts, paper, and shoes are important manufacturing industries. Boston, the largest city in New England, is a leading commercial and fishing port.

Did you know that Plymouth Rock, lobster, maple syrup, snow, and clam chowder are things commonly associated with this region? They are also related to the geography of New England, which includes rocky terrain, mountains, forests, a rugged coastline, and natural harbors.

Because of its location, the New England region has a cool, wet climate. The plants and animals found in this area are determined by both the climate and the soil.

U.S. Geography 4–5—RB-904003

Quick Facts

Capital: Augusta
Population: 1,274,923 (2000 census)
Area: 30,864 sq mi (79,939 sq km)
State Bird: chickadee
State Tree: eastern white pine
Statehood: 1820

MAINE

Augusta

Maine forms the northeastern corner of the United States. It is the largest state in New England. The Canadian provinces of Quebec and New Brunswick border Maine to the northwest and northeast. It is bordered by New Hampshire on the west and the Atlantic Ocean on the east. Because Maine was once covered by glaciers, it has a rocky and wild coast, which is one of the state's most breathtaking features. This state has nearly 600,000 acres of parkland made up of mountains, rivers, lakes, and woodlands. The jagged coastline, which is about 3,000 miles long, is longer than the coastline of California.

Mount Katahdin, Maine's tallest mountain, is 5,267 (1,605m) high. It is located in Baxter State Park and is the official end of the Appalachian Trail. Each year thousands of hikers travel along the 2,000 miles of trail between Springer Mountain in Georgia up to Maine. The second most visited park in the United States is Acadia National Park located on Mount Desert Island. Here you will find wild blueberries and stunning beaches. Also found on this island is Bar Harbor, where wealthy Americans such as J. P. Morgan and John D. Rockefeller owned mansions.

Comprehending Maine: Answer the following questions.

1. Maine can be found in the _____ corner of the U.S.

2. Maine's coastline is longer than the coastline of _____.

3. The second most visited park in the U.S. is _____.

4. _____ left Maine with a rocky and wild coast.

5. The area of Maine is _____ square miles.

4

Quick Facts

Capital: Concord
Population: 1,184,000 (2000 census)
Area: 8,969 sq mi (23,230 sq km)
State Bird: purple finch
State Tree: white birch
Statehood: 1788

NEW HAMPSHIRE

Concord

New Hampshire's nickname, "the Granite State," comes from the White Mountains, which are made of red and gray granite. These mountains run through the state. The highest peak, Mount Washington, is one of the windiest places on earth. The Old Man of the Mountain, a famous landmark, was a rock formation that looked like an old man's face. It became the official symbol of the state in 1945. Unfortunately, the formation recently fell. Lake Winnipesaukee is the largest of 1,300 lakes and ponds in the White Mountain National Forest.

At one time glaciers covered the state with huge sheets of ice about a mile thick. As the glaciers retreated, they left behind rocky soil. Lakes, ponds, hills, swamps, and bogs found in the state are the result of the glacial movement.

New Hampshire's thirteen-mile-long coastline is shorter than any other state that borders an ocean; however, the coastline contains many sandy beaches. Portsmouth is the state's port on the Atlantic Ocean. Even with its short coastline, New Hampshire became an important ship-building location.

Lumber, paper products, and wood pulp are produced by the people of this state. Machinery, electrical equipment, plastic, and fabricated metal products are also produced here. New Hampshire was at one time an agricultural state. There are still some dairy farms, but the state now makes more things rather than growing them.

Directions: Research to find more information about New Hampshire. Then make a travel brochure that might encourage others to visit the state.

Travel Today!

5

Quick Facts

Capital: Providence
Population: 1,048,319 (2000 census)
Area: 1,045 sq mi (2,706 sq km)
State Bird: Rhode Island Red chicken
State Tree: red maple
Statehood: 1790

The New England state of Rhode Island is not quite fifty miles wide, but its shoreline along the Atlantic Ocean measures approximately 500 miles. This is because the state includes over thirty islands. The largest of these is Aquidneck Island.

The harbors of Narragansett Bay were important to ship builders and whalers in the late 1600s and 1700s. Later, Rhode Island began to produce textiles and jewelry. It is still one of the main producers of silverware. Commercial fishing and tourism are important to the state's economy. Two important resort areas are Newport and Block Island. Today, agriculture does not play a large part in Rhode Island's economy; however, in 1895, the "Rhode Island Red" became recognized as a new breed of chicken. Farmers in the state were noted for raising chickens.

Testing Yourself: Choose the best answer for the questions below.

1. Two of Rhode Island's most important economic activities are
   A. textiles and jewelry.
   B. fishing and tourism.
   C. ship building and whaling.
   D. raising chickens and sailing.

2. There are how many islands in Rhode Island?
   A. less than 10
   B. 1,600
   C. more than 50
   D. over 30

3. A "Rhode Island Red" is a/an
   A. chicken.
   B. silverware.
   C. textile.
   D. island.

4. The largest island in Rhode Island is
   A. Narragansett.
   B. Rhode.
   C. Aquidneck.
   D. Newport.

Quick Facts

Capital: Hartford
Population: 3,405,565 (2000 census)
Area: 4,845 sq mi (12,549 sq km)
State Bird: American robin
State Tree: white oak
Statehood: 1788

Hartford ★

CONNECTICUT

Connecticut's name comes from an Algonquian Indian word that means "beside the long tidal river." The Connecticut River, which runs south to Long Island Sound in the Atlantic Ocean, divides the state in half. The coastline of Long Island Sound contains many streams, rivers, marshes, and coves. Connecticut has many waterfalls and fast-running streams that produce water power.

Connecticut leads New England in the production of peaches, pears, mushrooms, and eggs. It is the second largest producer of oysters in the nation. Many greenhouse and nursery agricultural products are grown and sold here, along with maple syrup and Christmas trees.

Factories in Connecticut produce jet engines, helicopters, weapons, cutlery, clocks, locks, silverware, and submarines. The first nuclear-powered submarine, the *Nautilus*, was built in Groton. Insurance is another important business in the state. There are more insurance companies in Hartford than anywhere else in the United States.

Creating a License Plate: Follow these simple directions.

Use a plain sheet of 8 1/2 x 11 paper and design a license plate for Connecticut. Decide what colors you will use for the letters, numbers, and background. Print the state's name and its nickname. You may want to include a picture that represents the state, such as the state tree, flower, bird, or symbol. After completing your license plate, write a brief description and give reasons why you chose to draw and design your license plate as you did.

© Rainbow Bridge Publishing

U.S. Geography 4–5—RB-904003

Quick Facts

Capital: Montpelier
Population: 608,827 (2000 census)
Area: 9,249 sq mi (23,955 sq km)
State Bird: hermit thrush
State Tree: sugar maple
Statehood: 1791

Montpelier ★

V E R M O N T

The name *Vermont* comes from French words meaning "green mountain." The Green Mountains, which are part of the Appalachian Mountains, run from north to south through the center of the state like a backbone. The tallest mountain, Mount Mansfield, stands 4,393 feet (1,340 m). The second tallest mountain is Camel's Hump, which is shaped like a camel's hump. Forests cover more than four and a half million acres of the state. Lake Champlain, which borders New York and Quebec, is the largest lake in Vermont.

Vermont is the largest producer of maple syrup in the United States. During the sugaring time, millions of trees are tapped to produce the annual syrup harvest. The maple trees also attract thousands of tourists who come in early October to see the magnificent leaves as they turn various shades of red and gold. Waterbury is the location of the original Ben & Jerry's Ice Cream Factory. Another industry in the state is granite and marble cutting. The Green Mountains are the source of these valuable rocks. The snow-capped peaks also attract skiers. The state's rugged, rocky terrain discourages farming, but raising fruit trees and dairy farming are successful enterprises.

Viewing Vermont: Answer the following questions.

1. _____is the location of the original Ben & Jerry's Ice Cream Factory.

2. Vermont is the largest producer of _____ _____ in the U.S.

3. Mount Mansfield is the _____ mountain in the state.

4. The population of Vermont is _____ in the 2000 census.

8

Massachusetts (MA)

Quick Facts

Capital: Boston
Population: 6,349,097 (2000 census)
Area: 7,838 sq mi (20,300 sq km)
State Bird: chickadee
State Tree: American elm
Statehood: 1788

MASSACHUSETTS

Boston

The eastern border of Massachusetts opens onto one bay or another, thus providing the nickname the Bay State. The Berkshire Hills are located in the western part of Massachusetts. These hills are part of the Taconic Mountains. Mount Greylock, the highest point in the state, is located here. The eastern part of the state consists of lowlands that lie close to the Atlantic coast. Here you will find many ponds and cranberry bogs.

There are two major influences on the climate of Massachusetts. The first is its location in the path of several storm patterns. The other is its close proximity to the ocean and the Gulf Stream. Because of this, temperatures in the eastern part of the state are milder than in the rest of the state.

The Connecticut River runs south through the state in a valley that contains rich, fertile soil. Farmers in the valley produce eggs, milk, cranberries, and many vegetables. The cranberry crop is the second largest in the United States. A large fishing industry is located here, with catches of flounder, cod, haddock, and clams. Dairy and poultry products and nursery and greenhouse produce are also important industries in the state.

Designing a Postcard: Follow these simple directions.

Research to learn more about Massachusetts. Design a postcard describing the state. On one side, draw a colorful picture of a famous landmark, a tourist attraction, or a geographic feature. On the other side, write a short note to a friend or relative describing the landmark, attraction, or feature. Then design a stamp to represent Massachusetts.

9

Directions: Use the map below and the information on the previous pages to complete the questions. In addition, locate and label the capital of each New England state.

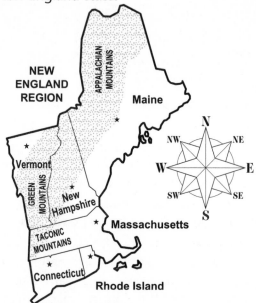

1. _____ is the mountain range that runs through much of New England.

2. In Vermont, the mountains are known as the _____ Mountains.

3. The country of _____ borders New England to the north.

4. _____ is located west of Maine and east of Vermont.

5. New England is located in the _____ part of the U.S.

6. _____ is the smallest state in New England.

7. Connecticut lies to the _____ of Massachusetts.

8. In Massachusetts, the Appalachians are known as the _____ Mountains.

Middle Atlantic Region

The Middle Atlantic region includes Maryland, Pennsylvania, New Jersey, New York, and Delaware. All five of the states in this region were original colonies of the United States. The Atlantic Coastal Plains and the Appalachian Mountains are the two predominant physical regions found within this area. In the Middle Atlantic region, there are more farm houses than office buildings, more fields than concrete roads, and more wooded hills than factory chimneys.

The Hudson River separates New York from New Jersey and empties into New York Bay and the Atlantic Ocean at New York City. After flowing southward through Pennsylvania and New Jersey, the Delaware River flows along the southeastern border of New York and Pennsylvania and into the Delaware Bay. This area is well known for its bays, deepwater harbors, lakes, and waterways, as well as its fertile hills, lowlands, and forest-covered mountains. In this region, temperatures fluctuate from season to season with a climate that is mostly moderate.

The Middle Atlantic states rank as the most densely populated area of the country. Three of the most populated states, New York, New Jersey, and Pennsylvania, are located here. The people in this region are engaged in tourism, service industries, international trade, and manufacturing. Steel, machinery, computers, and transportation equipment are some of the major products of this region. The transportation system, which includes roadways and trains, is quite extensive. New York, the nation's largest city, is considered the cultural center and the financial hub of the country. New York City also has the busiest port in the region.

Even though agriculture does not play a dominant economic role in the Middle Atlantic region, the main agricultural products include chickens, dairy products, fruits, and vegetables. Coal, clay, petroleum, sand, limestone, and gravel are some of this region's natural resources.

11

Quick Facts

Capital: Annapolis
Population: 5,296,486 (2000 census)
Area: 9,774 sq mi (25,316 sq km)
State Bird: Baltimore oriole
State Tree: white oak
Statehood: 1788

Maryland is an oddly shaped state; it is split into two uneven pieces by the Chesapeake Bay. The large Western Shore is made up of land between the Potomac River and the Chesapeake Bay. The small Eastern Shore shares the Delmarva Peninsula with Virginia and Delaware. The blue crabs of Maryland love the murky waters of Chesapeake Bay, which opens into the Atlantic Ocean. It is fed by four hundred miles of rivers. Crabs are a large part of the state's fishing industry. Fishing for crabs and other species in the tidal waters is a favorite pastime.

In western Maryland, the Allegheny Mountains are thickly forested. The highest point in the state is 3,360 feet (1,024 m) above sea level on Blackbone Mountain. The lowest point is a depression 174 feet (54 m) below sea level in the Chesapeake Bay called Bloody Point Hole.

Baltimore, the largest city, has one of the largest natural harbors in the world. Annapolis, the capital, sits along Chesapeake Bay. This bay, with its many inlets, is a popular vacation spot, offering excellent fishing and sailing.

Some of Maryland's tourist attractions are listed below. Research and identify each with a statement telling why it is popular.

1. Fort McHenry _____

2. Camden Yards _____

3. National Aquarium _____

4. Ocean City _____

Quick Facts

Capital: Harrisburg
Population: 12,281,054 (2000 census)
Area: 44,817 sq mi (116,082 sq km)
State Bird: ruffed grouse
State Tree: hemlock
Statehood: 1787

Pennsylvania, known as the Keystone State, received its name because of its location in the middle of the thirteen original states. With six states to the north and six to the south, it was the "keystone" in an arch of states. The state is bordered on the north by Lake Erie and New York, on the east by New Jersey, on the south by Delaware and Maryland, and on the south and west by West Virginia and Ohio. Pennsylvania ranks fifth in population and thirty-third in size. Pennsylvania is also known as the Quaker State because many of its founders were Quakers. One of the most famous Quakers was William Penn, who was awarded a land grant of twenty-eight million acres from the British king Charles II. Penn founded Philadelphia, the largest city in the state.

Manufacturing is the state's most important economic activity. Pennsylvania is a state of firsts for North America. Some of these firsts include the first ice cream soda, root beer, computer, electron microscope, oil well, cookbook, steamship, bifocal glasses, and steam locomotive.

Some fun places to visit in Pennsylvania are described below. Use a state map to locate these places. Then, write the names of each place next to the correct spot on the map.

Hershey is the chocolate capital of the nation.

Punxsutawney is famous for its Groundhog Festival.

Philadelphia is the home of the Liberty Bell.

Gettysburg was the site of one the Civil War's greatest battles.

Pittsburgh is the home of Three Rivers Stadium.

13

Quick Facts

Capital: Trenton
Population: 8,414,350 (2000 census)
Area: 7,787 sq mi (20,168 sq km)
State Bird: eastern goldfinch
State Tree: red oak
Statehood: 1787

Trenton

NEW JERSEY

New Jersey is nicknamed the **Garden State** because of its many fruit orchards and vegetable farms; however, most of the people live in metropolitan areas, and it is primarily an **industrial** state. Soon after becoming a state, New Jersey became an industrial leader. Ironwork and glass-making were two of the state's early industries. **Textiles** and paper products were industries that developed later. During the first half of the twentieth century, the state became a leading producer of ships and ammunition. Today, however, it is known for producing **chemicals**, electronic equipment, and **medicine**.

Many people come to the state to visit **Atlantic City**, **Menlo Park**, **Pine Barrens**, and several Revolutionary War sites. Lucy the Elephant is a six-story landmark in Margate. Tourists can climb a circular stair, sit in the maharajah's howdah, and view the ocean. A promoter built this landmark in 1882 to help advertise a real estate development.

New Jersey Jumble: Find the words shown in boldface in the word search puzzle. The words can run horizontally, vertically, or diagonally. Circle the answers.

```
s  l  a  c  i  m  e  h  c  m  e  j
l  m  m  e  d  i  c  i  n  e  c  c
g  a  r  d  e  n  s  t  a  t  e  g
y  t  i  c  c  i  t  n  a  l  t  a
s  e  l  i  t  x  e  t  q  b  a  j
f  y  e  b  z  e  i  m  p  q  f  v
z  p  o  k  r  a  p  o  l  n  e  m
l  a  i  r  t  s  u  d  n  i  w  w
u  j  q  d  y  q  g  e  u  z  o  e
s  n  e  r  r  a  b  e  n  i  p  b
f  h  u  t  c  u  j  u  k  g  m  u
f  y  e  s  r  e  j  w  e  n  l  g
```

14

New York (NY)

Quick Facts

Capital: Albany
Population: 18,976,457 (2000 census)
Area: 47,223 sq mi (122,309 sq km)
State Bird: bluebird
State Tree: sugar maple
Statehood: 1788

New York stretches from Lake Erie and Lake Ontario to the Atlantic Ocean. Sitting on the banks of Lake Erie is the city of Buffalo, known for its heavy snowfalls. Niagara Falls lies just to the north and is shared by the United States and Canada. Toward the east are New York's Finger Lakes, a group of eleven long, deep lakes. Located to the south are the Adirondack Mountains with forty-five peaks over 4,000 feet. The Hudson River flows out of the Adirondack Mountains, past the capital city of Albany, and through the Catskill Mountains. New York City, the largest city in population in the United States, is located in the southern part of the state. New York City, known as the Big Apple, is the center for banking and finance of the country. There are also many tourist attractions here, including the Empire State Building and the Statue of Liberty. The Empire State Building, at one time the tallest building in the world, gets its name from this state's nickname.

New York is a major clothing manufacturing and publishing state, although agriculture is also important. Fruit orchards, dairy farms, and vineyards are found throughout the state. The orchards of New York produce more apples than any other state except Washington.

Notes on New York: After reading the paragraphs above, complete the following sentences with the correct answer.

1. The _____ was once the tallest building in the world.
2. The city of _____ sits on the banks of Lake Erie.
3. New York City is known as the _____.
4. _____ is shared by the United States and Canada.
5. The Hudson River flows out of the _____.
6. Clothing and _____ are important industries in New York.

15

Quick Facts

Capital: Dover
Population: 783,600 (2000 census)
Area: 2,045 sq mi (5,297 sq km)
State Bird: blue hen chicken
State Tree: American holly
Statehood: 1787

Dover ★

DELAWARE

Delaware is called the First State because it was the first state to ratify the United States Constitution. Besides being the oldest state, it is also the second smallest state after Rhode Island. Delaware measures only 35 miles (56 kilometers) from east to west and only 96 miles (155 kilometers) from north to south. The eastern border is comprised of the Atlantic Ocean and the Delaware River. It is bordered to the west and south by Maryland and to the north by Pennsylvania.

The economy and industry of this state have been connected to one family in particular—the Du Ponts. In 1802, Eleuthere Du Pont started a company that made gunpowder. Today, the DuPont Company is still in business manufacturing chemicals. Wilmington, one of the state's largest cities, is home to the DuPont Company. DuPont also produces paint, synthetic fibers, dyes, and plastic. Fishing and tourism are also important to Delaware's economy. Over $4 million a year is brought into the state through commercial fishing. Menhaden, a type of herring, provide fish meal, oil, and fertilizers. Freshwater fishing is also a popular pastime.

Digging into Delaware! Match the places and things on the left with the descriptions on the right.

1. First State
2. menhaden
3. Wilmington
4. DuPont
5. fishing
6. Pennsylvania

A. one of the largest cities in Delaware
B. a type of herring
C. important to the state's economy
D. Delaware's nickname
E. borders Delaware to the north
F. company that produces chemicals

Middle Atlantic Puzzle

Complete the puzzle using the clues shown below.

Across

2. New York City's nickname
4. an oddly shaped state that is split into two uneven pieces
5. the nickname of New Jersey
9. This city is known as the chocolate capital of the nation.

Down

1. the person who founded the city of Philadelphia
3. the state capital of Pennsylvania
6. the First State
7. New York State is the second largest producer of these in the U.S.
8. Lucy the _____ is a six-story landmark in Margate, NJ.

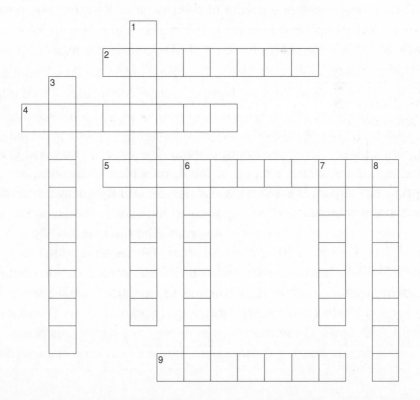

© Rainbow Bridge Publishing   U.S. Geography 4–5—RB-904003

Southeast Region

The Southeast region has become a manufacturing region, and high-rise buildings fill the skylines of cities such as Atlanta, Miami, Birmingham, and Charlotte. The region boasts a mild climate and plentiful rainfall. Because of its mild weather, the Southeast attracts many retirees from other regions.

For at least six months of the year, crops can be grown easily without danger of frost. The southern plateaus, with their fertile soil and warm climates, are perfect for growing numerous crops, including cotton, peaches, peanuts, and tobacco.

There are numerous rivers, lakes, and other large bodies of water in the Southeast region. Some of these have a tremendous influence on the climate, and others form borders between states. For example, the Mississippi River forms one border of West Virginia, Kentucky, Tennessee, Arkansas, Mississippi, and Louisiana. The region is also known for its coastline and beaches along the Gulf of Mexico and the Atlantic Ocean.

The Southeast region, including Georgia, South Carolina, Virginia, Florida, Alabama, West Virginia, North Carolina, Mississippi, Tennessee, Kentucky, Louisiana, and Arkansas, has a variety of geographic features. The land ranges from rugged mountains to sandy beaches, with rich valleys, fertile plains, and a piedmont plateau. The Great Smoky and Blue Ridge Mountains, which are part of the Appalachian Mountains, are found in this region. West Virginia, Tennessee, and Kentucky are landlocked states that contain the Appalachian highlands. The Ouachita and Ozark Mountains can be found in Arkansas. The discovery of the Cumberland Gap in 1750 opened Arkansas, Tennessee, and Kentucky to settlers. The southern lowlands are a humid, subtropical region containing many swamps, such as the Louisiana bayous, the Dismal Swamp of Virginia and North Carolina, the Florida Everglades, and the Okefenokee Swamp in Georgia. These marshy areas were once dangerous places filled with disease-bearing mosquitoes. They are now important wildlife refuges.

GEORGIA

Atlanta

Quick Facts

Capital: Atlanta
Population: 8,186,453 (2000 census)
Area: 58,918 sq mi (152,577 sq km)
State Bird: brown thrasher
State Tree: live oak
Statehood: 1788

Georgia is home to magnolias, peaches, old plantations, pecans, sandy beaches, and Southern hospitality. Agriculture in Georgia today is no longer dependent only on cotton. Georgians also raise poultry, hogs, and cattle.

Georgia, the largest state east of the Mississippi River, is almost equal to the size of the New England states combined. Atlanta, the capital and largest city, is the financial and commercial center of the Southeast Region and one of the fastest growing cities in the nation.

Tourism is an important industry in Georgia. Visitors come to see many attractions, including Stone Mountain Park, the Little White House, Callaway Gardens, Six Flags Over Georgia®, and various Civil War and historic sites such as Savannah and Brunswick. People also come to enjoy the mild climate and to relax on the coastal islands.

The northeastern part of Georgia includes a region of dense pine forest where the Blue Ridge Mountains rise. This region attracts tourists, hunters, and fishermen and provides valuable timber. The highest point in the state, Brasstown Bald, is located near the North Carolina–Georgia border. To the west of the mountains is the fertile Appalachian Valley, and to the south is the Piedmont, a plateau including Atlanta and many large farms. The largest areas of the state are the coastal plains where the Okefenokee Swamp is located.

Here is an important emblem found on the state flag. Use an encyclopedia or other resources to find the meaning of this emblem.

The meaning of the state seal of Georgia is

_____.

U.S. Geography 4–5—RB-904003

South Carolina (SC)

Quick Facts

Capital: Columbia
Population: 4,012,012 (2000 census)
Area: 30,111 sq mi (77,987 sq km)
State Bird: Carolina wren
State Tree: palmetto
Statehood: 1788

South Carolina, the smallest state in the "deep South," has a warm climate, rolling green hills, the Appalachian Mountains, and miles of white sandy beaches. It is bordered by Georgia to the southwest and North Carolina to the north and northeast. The state ranks fortieth in size. There are three main geographic regions: the Atlantic Coastal Plain, the Blue Ridge Region, and the Piedmont. Sassafras Mountain, the highest point in South Carolina, is located in the northwest corner near the North Carolina and Georgia borders.

The Congaree National Park is found southeast of the capital city of Columbia. Over 21,000 acres were designated as a national monument in 1976 to preserve this tract of land, which is the last significant area containing river-bottom hardwood trees. There are over ninety species of trees in this area. Congaree was designated a national park in 2003.

Service and manufacturing have become more important to the state's economy than agriculture. Chemicals, paper, and textile production are important industries along with tourism. Hilton Head Island and Myrtle Beach are just two of the resorts that attract vacationers to this state's coast. The agricultural industry produces crops such as peaches, corn, wheat, cotton, tobacco, soybeans, and tomatoes.

Studying South Carolina: Answer the following questions.

1. _____ Mountain is the highest point in the state.

2. South Carolina ranks _____ in size.

3. Congaree National Park is found _____ of Columbia.

4. _____ and _____ are two of the resorts that attract vacationers to the state.

Quick Facts

Capital: Richmond
Population: 7,078,515 (2000 census)
Area: 39,597 sq mi (102,558 sq km)
State Bird: cardinal
State Tree: dogwood
Statehood: 1788

VIRGINIA
Richmond *

Agriculture has always been an important part of the economy of Virginia. Tobacco was and is the state's main crop. Other farm products include vegetables, cattle, hay, chickens, and dairy products. The Shenandoah Valley contains the most fertile soil. It is a major apple growing region in the United States. Most of the money from agriculture comes from raising cattle and poultry and dairy farming. More turkeys are produced in Rockingham County than most other places in the U.S.

The state of Virginia extends from the Chesapeake Bay in the east to the Allegheny Mountains in the west. There are several land regions, including the Blue Ridge Mountains, the Piedmont Plateau, and the Tidewater area, or coastal plain. The Potomac, James, Rappahannock, and York Rivers, which are found in the Tidewater region, empty into the Chesapeake Bay.

Many residents of Virginia work for the federal government in Washington, D.C. Others are employed at various military installations in the state. Trade, manufacturing, and services are other ways of earning an income in Virginia.

Viewing Virginia: Match the description with the places or things.

1. This is the main crop of Virginia.

2. The most fertile soil is found here.

3. Turkeys are grown here.

4. The coastal plains are found here.

5. This is the state bird of Virginia.

A. Shenandoah Valley

B. Rockingham County

C. cardinal

D. Tidewater region

E. tobacco

U.S. Geography 4–5—RB-904003

Quick Facts

Capital: Tallahassee
Population: 15,982,378 (2000 census)
Area: 53,997 sq mi (139,853 sq km)
State Bird: mockingbird
State Tree: sabal palmetto palm
Statehood: 1845

Vacationers flock to the Sunshine State each year because of its warm climate, even though the state is often hit by hurricanes. Florida is also struck by lightning more often than any other state. Despite these threats from nature, tourism is Florida's largest industry.

Walt Disney World in Orlando is one of the top vacation spots in the world. Here you can find four theme parks: Epcot, Disney-MGM Studios, Magic Kingdom, and Animal Kingdom. Not too far away are Sea World and Universal Studios. Further east, tourists visit Cape Canaveral and Kennedy Space Center. The oldest city in the United States, St. Augustine, can be found to the north along the Atlantic coast. Further south in Daytona Beach, tourists can visit the Daytona International Speedway. If you travel west from Daytona, you can enjoy Busch Gardens in Tampa. If you travel south to Miami, you can immerse yourself in Cuban culture. Travelers to the Sunshine State will find plenty of places to visit and things to do.

Use the clues below and the information written above to name tourist attractions in Florida. Use an atlas to help you mark the cities on the map.

1. the state capital
2. the home of Mickey Mouse
3. place immersed in Cuban culture
4. Busch Gardens is located here.
5. Astronauts are launched from here.
6. oldest city in the United States
7. city famous for car races

22

Montgomery•
ALABAMA

Quick Facts

Capital: Montgomery
Population: 4,447,100 (2000 census)
Area: 50,750 sq mi (131,443 sq km)
State Bird: yellowhammer
State Tree: southern longleaf pine
Statehood: 1819

Except for a short coastline along the Gulf of Mexico, this state is mostly landlocked and is largely rectangular. To the north is Tennessee; to the east is Georgia; to the south is Florida; and to the west is Mississippi. The highest point in Alabama is Cheaha Mountain, located in the eastern part of the state. The lowest elevation is along the Gulf of Mexico.

Cotton was the only major crop in the state for many years; today, however, manufacturing dominates the economy. Chemical products, paper, metals, and textiles are just some of Alabama's products. Birmingham, the largest city, is a center for commerce and industry. A valuable seaport, Mobile, is located at the mouth of the Mobile River. Marshall Space Flight Center, one of NASA's (National Aeronautics and Space Administration) largest facilities, is located in Huntsville.

Many famous people have called Alabama home. One of the state's most noted citizens was Helen Keller. As a young child, she lost her sight and hearing. Helen Keller demonstrated the capabilities of the physically challenged through her lectures and writings. Another well-known citizen was George Washington Carver, who developed more than 300 products and uses for the soybean, the sweet potato, and the peanut.

Use the information above and other resources to match the following famous Alabamians with their descriptions.

1. George Washington Carver   **A.** lost her sight and hearing

2. Jesse Owens   **B.** called the "Father of the Blues"

3. Helen Keller   **C.** developed over 300 products

4. Clifton C. Williams   **D.** the first astronaut from Alabama

5. W. C. Handy   **E.** won a gold medal in the 1936 Berlin Olympics

U.S. Geography 4–5—RB-904003

Quick Facts

Capital: Charleston
Population: 1,808,344 (2000 census)
Area: 24,086 sq mi (62,384 sq km)
State Bird: cardinal
State Tree: sugar maple
Statehood: 1863

West Virginia was originally part of the state of Virginia. It is a landlocked state, which means it does not have a coast. The state is located east of Ohio and Kentucky, south of Maryland and Pennsylvania, and west of Virginia. It has two peninsulas, one extending to the north and the other to the northeast.

In 1609, James I, the king of England, gave this region to English settlers. The territory was not settled until 1726, however. Shepherdstown, founded in 1727, claims to be the first permanent settlement. In 1742, George Washington surveyed land in what would become West Virginia. The Cherokee and Iroquois Indians gave up claims to the land in 1770. The last battle of the Revolutionary War occurred at Wheeling in 1782 when the colonists defeated a British and Indian attack on Fort Henry. Harper's Ferry became a U.S. arsenal in 1796. John Brown, an abolitionist, seized the arsenal in 1859. West Virginia separated from Virginia in 1861. In 1863, West Virginia became the thirty-fifth state.

Today the main industries in West Virginia are tourism, mining, manufacturing, and services. Chemicals, machinery, aluminum, plastic, and hardwood products are produced in West Virginia. This state is one of the top three coal producers in the United States. Skiing, rafting, hiking, hunting, and fishing attract thousands of tourists each year.

West Virginia is called the Mountain State because it is entirely within the Appalachian Mountain Range. It has the highest average elevation of all states east of the Mississippi River. Its highest point, Spruce Knob, is located in the Allegheny Plateau.

On a separate sheet of paper, use the dates and brief descriptions above to create a timeline. Your timeline should contain ten entries.

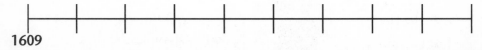

1609

Quick Facts

Capital: Raleigh
Population: 8,049,313 (2000 census)
Area: 48,718 sq mi (126,179 sq km)
State Bird: cardinal
State Tree: pine
Statehood: 1789

According to one story, North Carolina is called the Tar Heel State because some of its residents poured tar from pine trees into a river to slow down British troops during the American Revolution. The name *Carolina* comes from a Latin word for Charles. The state's name honors King Charles I of England. The capital city, Raleigh, was named after the English explorer Sir Walter Raleigh.

The history of this state is particularly interesting because many pirates used the coast for a refuge. The infamous pirate Blackbeard roamed this area until he died in 1718. Other pirates—including two women, Anne Bonney and Mary Read—also used the area as their headquarters.

The Piedmont region of North Carolina has a thriving poultry industry. Tobacco is the main crop grown along the coastal plains. Other crops grown in the state include wheat, peanuts, sweet potatoes, and cotton. The state is also a center for textiles, machinery, metal, and food processing. Charlotte, the largest city, is a major financial center.

Knowing North Carolina. Read the following questions and choose the best answer.

1. The state's name honors
   A. Charlotte.
   B. King Charles I.
   C. Blackbeard.
   D. Mary Read.

2. The main crop grown along the coastal plains is
   A. wheat.
   B. sweet potatoes.
   C. tobacco.
   D. peanuts.

3. The capital of North Carolina is
   A. Charlotte.
   B. Raleigh.
   C. Charles.
   D. Piedmont.

U.S. Geography 4–5—RB-904003

Quick Facts

Capital: Jackson
Population: 2,844,658 (2000 census)
Area: 46,913 sq mi (121,506 sq km)
State Bird: mockingbird
State Tree: magnolia
Statehood: 1817

Mississippi has large forest resources because most of the state is covered with trees suitable for lumbering. There are also petroleum and natural gas deposits. The Yazoo, Pearl, and Tennessee Rivers provide important recreation and hydroelectric facilities. Of course, the most famous river in the state is the one that shares its name, the Mississippi, which means "father of waters."

Many famous musicians have come from the state of Mississippi. B. B. King and Muddy Waters were some of the originators of the "Delta Blues." Elvis Presley, a rock-and-roll singer, was born in Tupelo. Country singers Tammy Wynette, LeAnn Rimes, and Charley Pride are other famous musicians from Mississippi. Although not a singer, Oprah Winfrey is another well-known person from Mississippi.

Create a State Mobile Directions: Use a variety of resources to make a mobile about the state of Mississippi. You will need the following materials: construction paper, yarn or string, markers or colored pencils, glue or a glue stick, scissors, and coat hangers.

1. Cut about ten shapes (squares, rectangles, circles, etc.) from the construction paper.
2. Draw or cut out pictures of important people, places, or things that describe Mississippi.
3. Glue pictures onto each of the shapes.
4. Write a description or a fact on the back of the construction paper.
5. Punch a hole in each shape. Then cut pieces of yarn or string and attach to each shape.
6. Hang the pictures from the coat hangers at different levels to create a mobile about Mississippi.
7. Make a sign to attach to the top of the mobile to identify the state.

Quick Facts

Capital: Nashville
Population: 5,689,283 (2000 census)
Area: 41,219 sq mi (106,758 sq km)
State Bird: mockingbird
State Tree: tulip poplar
Statehood: 1796

Nashville

TENNESSEE

Tennessee stretches about 480 miles (770 km) from the Appalachian Mountains in the east to the Mississippi River in the west. The state is bordered by Virginia and Kentucky to the north, North Carolina to the east, Missouri and Arkansas to the west, and Alabama, Mississippi, and Georgia to the south. Tennessee was nicknamed the Volunteer State because it sent a large number of soldiers to the Revolutionary War, the War of 1812, the Mexican War, and the Civil War.

Millions of visitors come to the Great Smoky Mountains National Park each year. Near Jackson, Pinson Mounds is an outstanding archaeological site that contains the remains of an Indian city. Other tourist attractions in the state include the Grand Ole Opry in Nashville; Graceland, the home of Elvis Presley, in Memphis; and the Hermitage, home of former president Andrew Jackson, near Nashville. The state also has several Civil War battlefields, including Shiloh, Lookout Mountain, and Chickamauga.

Because of its mild climate and plentiful rainfall, farmers in this state are able to grow many food products. Some of the main agricultural products include cattle, dairy products, soybeans, cotton, corn, and tobacco. A famous breed of saddlehorse named after the state is raised here. Some of the leading industries in Tennessee are chemicals, publishing, printing, food products, transportation equipment, and machinery.

Tracking Tennessee: Answer the following questions.

1. The _____ attract millions of visitors each year.
2. Farmers are able to produce many food products because of the _____ and _____
3. _____ is the home of Elvis Presley located in Memphis.
4. Tennessee is bordered by _____ to the east.

Quick Facts

Capital: Frankfort
Population: 4,041,769 (2000 census)
Area: 39,732 sq mi (102,906 sq km)
State Bird: cardinal
State Tree: tulip poplar
Statehood: 1792

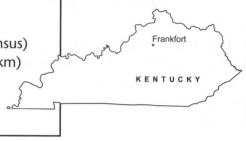

Kentucky's nickname, the Bluegrass State, comes from the bluish-green grass that is a source of food for livestock, especially the state's famous horses. The state ranks first in the breeding of thoroughbred horses. Located in the heart of the Bluegrass region, Louisville is sometimes called the "Horse Capital of the World." One of the most famous horse races in the world, the Kentucky Derby, is held each year in Louisville at Churchill Downs.

Kentucky is one of the nation's leading producers of coal, with mines both underground and on the surface. Other important minerals in Kentucky include petroleum, natural gas, gravel, clay, and stone. Steel, aluminum, machinery, automobiles, and chemicals are some of the leading types of manufacturing in the state.

A famous prize fighter, Muhammad Ali, came from Kentucky. Daniel Boone, a well-known explorer, blazed the Wilderness Trail through the Cumberland Gap in 1775. Abraham Lincoln and Zachary Taylor, two former presidents, also came from this state. Casey Jones, a famous train engineer, and Diane Sawyer, a well-known newscaster, also called Kentucky their home.

Directions: Write the answers to the following questions in the blanks on the right. Use the circled letters to spell the state's nickname.

1. famous horse race
2. Horse Capital of the World
3. a type of manufacturing
4. Muhammad Ali
5. former president
6. train engineer
7. newscaster

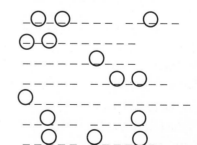

28

Louisiana (LA)

Quick Facts

Capital: Baton Rouge
Population: 4,468,976 (2000 census)
Area: 43,566 sq mi (112,836 sq km)
State Bird: brown pelican
State Tree: bald cypress
Statehood: 1812

Shaped like a capital "L," Louisiana is found entirely within the Gulf Coastal Plain. Louisiana is bordered by the Gulf of Mexico to the south, Texas to the west, Arkansas to the north, and Mississippi to the east. The most important rivers in Louisiana are the Red River, the Atchafalaya River, the Ouachita River, and the Mississippi River. In fact, much of this state's terrain is related to the Mississippi River.

Louisiana has a humid, subtropical climate throughout the state. It receives between forty-six and sixty-four inches of rain each year. Because of its warm, wet climate, agriculture has played an important part in this state's economy. Some of the main crops produced here include soybeans, sugar, sugar cane, rice, cotton, and hot peppers. Numerous varieties of fish and seafood are caught and sold in the state.

New Orleans is considered the state's most important tourist attraction because of the French Quarter, the Garden District, Lafayette Cemetery, and Jackson Square. In addition, the city attracts numerous visitors during the Mardi Gras celebration and is famous for its Dixieland jazz.

A Look at Louisiana: Answer the following multiple choice questions.

1. This city is Louisiana's most important tourist attraction.
   - **A.** Lafayette
   - **B.** New Orleans
   - **C.** Baton Rouge
   - **D.** Jackson
2. Much of the state's terrain is related to this river.
   - **A.** Atchafalaya
   - **B.** Red River
   - **C.** Ouachita
   - **D.** Mississippi
3. The state bird is the
   - **A.** bald cypress.
   - **B.** hot pepper.
   - **C.** brown pelican.
   - **D.** Lafayette.

29

Quick Facts

Capital: Little Rock
Population: 2,673,400 (2000 census)
Area: 52,075 sq mi (134,875 sq km)
State Bird: mockingbird
State Tree: pine
Statehood: 1836

Arkansas' nickname, the **Natural State**, comes from the appeal of its great outdoors and its many geological wonders. The **Ouachita Mountains**, located in the central and southwest region of the state, are a popular destination. **Magazine Mountain**, the highest point in the state, is found here. Also located in the foothills of the Ouachita Mountains is **Hot Springs** National Park. These springs have an average temperature of 143° F (62° C). One of the largest resort towns, Eureka Springs, is cut into the side of a mountain.

Arkansas is rich in minerals, especially **bauxite**, which is used to produce **aluminum**. Coal, natural gas, and **diamonds** are also found in Arkansas. The farms and forests provide the raw materials for many of the state's industries.

Many famous people have come from the state of Arkansas. Among them are author **Maya Angelou**, singer **Johnny Cash**, and five-star general Douglas MacArthur. Perhaps one of the most famous is former governor of the state and forty-second United States president, William J. **Clinton**.

Arkansas Jumble: Locate the words shown in boldface above in the word search puzzle.

```
b o t o w t d o c k n u m c x s r
p m r r j m i u x v n i a t a j d
a t f r e n a a f j i d y i s s g
l l v x t a m c z v a y a r u g s
u l n z m t o h s a t h a s o n u
m l j v t u n i a y n l n r t i n
i t o b b r d t s q u t g f k r n
n r h a v a s a x u o u e u d p o
u k n u b l z m c d m i l x x s t
m k n x m s q o g w e k o g l t n
i b y i s t w u a j n x u v r o i
p u c t h a v n s m i s z q d h l
b m a e k t c t l r z o t g a u c
j w s x l e p a a n a e o n m g t
e q h j s z f i b q g f c x u q f
h i w r x t s n m a a z m v v w z
e j r z w y e s v r m a m p h e b
```

Southeastern Nicknames

Directions: Each state has a nickname. See how many of the Southeastern states' nicknames you can match correctly.

_____ **1.** Georgia   **A.** The Heart of Dixie

_____ **2.** South Carolina   **B.** Natural State

_____ **3.** Virginia   **C.** Bluegrass State

_____ **4.** Florida   **D.** Peach State

_____ **5.** Alabama   **E.** Volunteer State

_____ **6.** West Virginia   **F.** Tar Heel State

_____ **7.** North Carolina   **G.** Palmetto State

_____ **8.** Mississippi   **H.** Pelican State

_____ **9.** Tennessee   **I.** Old Dominion State

_____ **10.** Kentucky   **J.** Magnolia State

_____ **11.** Louisiana   **K.** Mountain State

_____ **12.** Arkansas   **L.** Sunshine State

31

Plains Region

The Plains region includes Nebraska, Iowa, Missouri, North Dakota, Kansas, and South Dakota. Sometimes this region is known as the "Prairie." The states in this region have much in common. The land is mostly grassland with few trees and an elevation well above sea level.

The Plains region is important for food production. The black and dark brown soils support crops of grain, which in turn are used to raise beef and dairy cattle, turkeys, and hogs. Crops grown in this region include hay, corn, oats, wheat, barley, sunflowers, soybeans, and alfalfa. Iowa and parts of South Dakota, Nebraska, Kansas, and Missouri are all a part of an area known as the "Corn Belt." Much of the corn and soybeans produced in the U.S. come from this region.

The Missouri and Mississippi Rivers and their tributaries have been important for transporting goods and people in this area. These rivers have also been used to help irrigate farmland and to produce hydro-electric power.

The Plains region is located in the middle of North America. In order to survive, the animals that live here must be able to eat mainly grasses and flowering plants. They must also adapt to the climate. Rain comes seasonally, and temperatures vary drastically from season to season.

Parts of the Plains region are also known for mineral deposits. Oil and natural gas fields are found here. There are also deposits of gold, salt, coal, lead, and zinc.

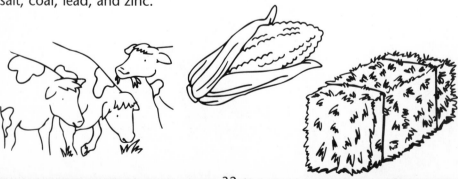

Nebraska (NE)

Quick Facts

Capital: Lincoln
Population: 1,711,263 (2000 census)
Area: 76,877 sq mi (199,113 sq km)
State Bird: western meadowlark
State Tree: cottonwood
Statehood: 1867

Nebraska is called the Cornhusker State because corn is one of its main crops. Over half of the state's population works in agriculture-related jobs.

Nebraska comes from the Otoe Indian word *nebrathka*, which means "flat water." This name refers to the Platte River, which runs across the state. The Missouri River forms the border between Nebraska and Iowa. At one time, the state was called the Tree Planters State because of early pioneers' efforts to plant trees on the prairie.

Blizzards in the winter and droughts in the summer are common for Nebraska. This state has light yearly precipitation and normally low humidity. Fortunately, there is a large supply of underground water available to irrigate the land.

Graphing Nebraska: Use the table showing Nebraska's population from 1900 to 2000 to plot the state's population on the line graph.

Year	Population
2000	1,711,000
1990	1,578,000
1980	1,570,000
1970	1,483,000
1960	1,411,000
1950	1,326,000
1940	1,316,000
1930	1,378,000
1920	1,296,000
1910	1,192,000
1900	1,066,000

33

Iowa (IA)

Quick Facts

Capital: Des Moines
Population: 2,926,324 (2000 census)
Area: 55,874 sq mi (144,716 sq km)
State Bird: eastern goldfinch
State Tree: oak
Statehood: 1846

The state's nickname, the Hawkeye State, honors a Sauk Indian chief, Black Hawk, who led a war against settlers in the Black Hawk War. Other nicknames, such as Land Where the Tall Corn Grows and the Corn State, refer to the state's leading farm crop. About eight percent of the food supply of the United States comes from Iowa.

Approximately ninety percent of the state is farmland made of fertile, black soil. Iowa is the world's largest producer of alfalfa, a plant in the pea family. In addition to alfalfa, Iowa is also the pig-farming capital of the world and a major producer of beef and pork. As a matter of fact, the World Pork Expo is held every year in the capital city of Des Moines.

The late actor John Wayne was among many famous Iowans. The Ringling brothers started their backyard circuses in McGregor, Iowa. Former President Herbert Hoover, the thirty-first president, was born in West Branch, Iowa.

Investigating Iowa: Answer the following fill-in-the-blank questions.

1. About _____ percent of the state is farmland.

2. The _____ is held every year in Des Moines.

3. _____, the thirty-first president, was born in Iowa.

4. The state bird of Iowa is the _____.

5. Iowa is the world's largest producer of _____.

6. _____ State is Iowa's nickname.

7. The state capital is the city of _____.

34

Missouri (MO)

Quick Facts

Capital: Jefferson City
Population: 5,595,211 (2000 census)
Area: 68,898 sq mi (178,446 sq km)
State Bird: bluebird
State Tree: dogwood
Statehood: 1821

Missouri is bordered by Iowa to the north, Illinois, Kentucky, and Tennessee to the east, Arkansas to the south, and Oklahoma, Kansas, and Nebraska to the west. The Mississippi River forms the state's eastern border. The upper western border is formed by the Missouri River, which continues through the state to join the Mississippi River. The most important inland port on the Mississippi River is the city of St. Louis, located ten miles south of the intersection of the Missouri and Mississippi Rivers.

The Gateway Arch in St. Louis, Missouri's largest city, is a famous stainless steel arch built to honor pioneers who passed through on their way west. The arch is the tallest monument in the United States. The Museum of Westward Expansion is located at the base of the monument.

The Ozark Plateau is located in the southern part of the state. The land in this region contains hilly forests and low mountains. Thousands of caves found here were once used as shelter by outlaws. This region attracts many tourists, especially fishermen because of a chain of lakes including Bull Shoals and Table Rock.

Molding Missouri: Use multicolored clay, a landform map of Missouri, toothpicks, labels, and glue to create a model of Missouri landforms. Use an 8 ½" x 11" piece of heavy cardboard to mount your clay model. Follow these simple directions:

1. Form the clay in the shape of the state of Missouri.
2. Use different colors of clay to form mountains, plateaus, rivers, and other landforms.
3. Insert toothpicks into the clay and attach labels to identify the various landforms.
4. Create a key to identify which colors of clay correspond to the various landforms.

© Rainbow Bridge Publishing U.S. Geography 4–5—RB-904003

Quick Facts

Capital: Bismarck
Population: 642,200 (2000 census)
Area: 70,704 sq mi (183,122 sq km)
State Bird: western meadowlark
State Tree: American elm
Statehood: 1889

NORTH DAKOTA
★Bismarck

North Dakota's name comes from the Dakota Indians, whose name means "friends" or "allies." The state's official nickname, the Peace Garden State, is in honor of the International Peace Garden located on its border with Canada. The state is sometimes known as the Flickertail State because of the Richardson ground squirrel, a type of squirrel or gopher that is abundant in the state.

The major industry in the state is agriculture. North Dakota's main crops include wheat, sunflowers, and barley. The richest farmland in North Dakota is found in the Red River Valley and on the plains. The second largest industry in the state is mining, and the largest coal reserves in the U.S. are found here.

North Dakota has a prairie in the east that rises to a high plateau in the west. The eastern part of the state is great for farming. The western part is too dry for farming, but beef cattle do well here. The Badlands, named by pioneers who faced difficulties crossing this region, are located in the west. In the Badlands, one can see strange land formations formed over millions of years by the erosion of soft rock.

Directions: Use the information above to match the description with the correct answer on the left.

1. Badlands	A. state capital
2. Red River Valley	B. located on the border of Canada
3. agriculture	C. named by the pioneers
4. Peace Garden	D. flickertail
5. prairie	E. area of rich farmland
6. Bismarck	F. rises to a high plateau
7. allies	G. major industry
8. squirrel	H. meaning of *Dakota*

Quick Facts

Capital: Topeka
Population: 2,688,418 (2000 census)
Area: 82,282 sq mi (213,109 sq km)
State Bird: western meadowlark
State Tree: cottonwood
Statehood: 1861

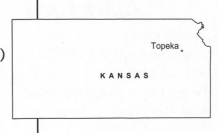

Topeka

KANSAS

Abilene, Dodge City, and Wichita became well-known cowtowns in the "**Old West**." **Dodge City** became the most notorious, with such characters as Doc Holliday, **Wyatt Earp**, and Bat Masterson. Major cattle drives crossed Kansas as cowboys moved herds of cattle from ranches in Texas to processing plants in Kansas.

One of Kansas's nicknames is the **Bread Basket** of America because it is the leading producer of **wheat** in the U.S. Sorghum and corn are also widely grown in the state. Its official nickname, the **Sunflower State**, refers to the wild flowers that once covered the prairies. Though Kansas is a top wheat producer, water is very scarce. Reasons for Kansas's success in agriculture include **irrigation** and its rich soil.

Kansas is a leading manufacturer of **aircraft**. **Wichita**, the largest city, produces private aircraft and aircraft parts. **Amelia Earhart**, born in Atchison, Kansas, was the first woman to fly an airplane across the Atlantic.

Kansas Jumble: Locate the words shown in boldface above in the word search puzzle. The words can be found horizontally, vertically, or diagonally.

```
a g t f a r c r i a i y z k c
n b w e x e s b v b q g x f f
j a t y o u z e u e n l m a p
t e k s a b d a e r b w h j d
n g x f q t x p b v r u s i o
q r g m d f t s s a z s o u g
r e t a t s r e w o l f n u s
v g z w g p k z a n w j s i v
f n o s b g z b u r w p x j w
q p u w i c h i t a p h n x h
x j r k v q p i c s w i e q j
t r a h r a e a i l e m a a s
h c q v f i x t s e w d l o t
y v s i r r i g a t i o n s w
y t i c e g d o d u i v p a o
```

37

South Dakota (SD)

Quick Facts

Capital: Pierre
Population: 754,844 (2000 Census)
Area: 75,896 sq mi (196,570 sq km)
State Bird: ring-necked pheasant
State Tree: Black Hills spruce
Statehood: 1889

SOUTH DAKOTA

Pierre *

The official nickname for South Dakota, Mount Rushmore State, comes from the famous national memorial found in the Black Hills. It has also been called the Land of Infinite Variety because of the various land-forms throughout the state. Over ninety percent of South Dakota is suitable for farming, but the state suffers from frequent frosts, droughts, and blizzards. Because of the blizzards, another nickname is the Blizzard State. It is also commonly referred to as the Coyote State because coyotes are native to the state.

South Dakota has two main land regions. In the eastern part of the state, farmers grow wheat, corn, alfalfa, and soybeans. To the west is a low mountain range known as the Black Hills. This famous mountain range contains sculptures of four presidents: George Washington, Thomas Jefferson, Abraham Lincoln, and Theodore Roosevelt. Beside the Black Hills is an area known as the Badlands, which contains ravines and jagged cliffs. The largest area of the Badlands is located between the Cheyenne and White Rivers. Beds of fossils dating back millions of years are found in Badlands National Park.

Studying South Dakota: Choose the best answer.

1. The area between the Cheyenne and White Rivers is called
   A. Black Hills.   C. Mount Rushmore.
   B. Badlands.   D. Coyote.

2. Which president is not carved in Mount Rushmore?
   A. Thomas Jefferson   C. Abraham Lincoln
   B. George Washington   D. Franklin Roosevelt

3. All of these are grown in the eastern part of the state except
   A. corn.   C. peanuts.
   B. soybeans.   D. wheat.

38

Graphing the Crops

Directions: Study the graph to answer the following questions.

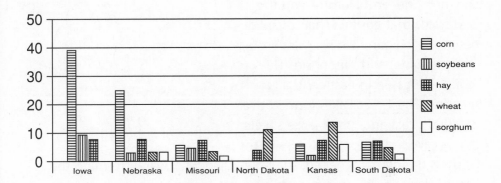

1. How many crops are grown in the Plains region?
   A. six
   C. twenty-four
   B. five
   D. forty

2. Which state grows the most corn?
   A. Iowa
   C. Kansas
   B. Nebraska
   D. South Dakota

3. Which state only grows hay and wheat?
   A. Kansas
   C. Iowa
   B. South Dakota
   D. North Dakota

4. Which state grows the most wheat?
   A. Nebraska
   C. Kansas
   B. North Dakota
   D. Iowa

5. About how much corn is grown in Iowa?
   A. 8 million tons
   C. 23 million tons
   B. 39 million tons
   D. 7 million tons

6. Of the following states, which grows the least sorghum?
   A. Nebraska
   C. Missouri
   B. Kansas
   D. South Dakota

U.S. Geography 4–5—RB-904003

Great Lakes Region

The Great Lakes region includes the Great Lakes—Ontario, Michigan, Superior, Erie, and Huron—and the U.S. states that contain their drainage basins—Michigan, Illinois, Minnesota, Ohio, Indiana, and Wisconsin. This region is located in east-central North America. The Great Lakes formed over 250,000 years ago when large sheets of ice, called glaciers, dug holes in the land. As the glaciers melted, the holes filled with water, forming the Great Lakes. These are the world's largest group of fresh water lakes and contain about 18 percent of the world's fresh water supply. These lakes cover an area of more than 750 miles (1,200 km) from west to east, and they have provided water for consumption, recreation, transportation, and power. The climates range from sub-arctic in the north to humid continental in the south and are moderated by the Great Lakes.

The Great Lakes Basin is home to more than one-tenth of the population of the United States. Some of the world's largest industrial concentrations are located in the Great Lakes region. The United States considers this region as a fourth seacoast.

In the late 1700s, new Americans of European descent began to settle on the south shores of Lake Ontario and Lake Erie. In 1835, settlements spread across southern Michigan, northern Ohio, Indiana, Illinois, and into southern Wisconsin. The entire region was settled by 1890 except for a part of Minnesota north of Duluth. The settlement brought major changes to the region. Forests were cut down to allow for farming. The lumber was used for fuel. Many streams were dammed to provide water power for mills and other industries.

Eastern white pine forests were clear-cut for lumber from 1850 through 1890 in the lower peninsula of Michigan and northern Wisconsin. During that same time period, large forest fires raged in this region. Native animals were also affected by the settlements, and many species became extinct.

www.summerbridgeactivities.com   © Rainbow Bridge Publishing

Michigan (MI)

Wolverine State

Quick Facts

Capital: Lansing
Population: 9,938,444 (2000 census)
Area: 56,809 sq mi (147,135 sq km)
State Bird: robin
State Tree: white pine
Statehood: 1837

The two peninsulas that comprise the state of Michigan are bordered by four of the five Great Lakes: Erie, Huron, Superior, and Michigan. The Lower Peninsula is larger and more populated than the Upper Peninsula, which is more wild and rugged. One of the world's largest suspension bridges, Mackinac Bridge, is located in Michigan.

Detroit, the largest city in Michigan, is often called "Motor City" because Henry Ford invented the assembly line here, allowing carmakers to create cars at a faster pace. Detroit is also the home of Motown Records, started by Berry Gordy. During the 1960s and '70s, Motown dominated the pop music scene with such stars as Diana Ross and Stevie Wonder.

Directions: Study the map of Michigan and then answer the questions.

1. Is Mt. Arvon found in the Upper or Lower Peninsula?

   _____

2. Name two states that border Michigan. _____

   _____

3. Lansing is located along the _____ River.

4. Battle Creek is _____ (direction) of Flint.

41

© Rainbow Bridge Publishing

U.S. Geography 4–5—RB-904003

Illinois (IL)

Quick Facts

Capital: Springfield
Population: 12,419,293 (2000 census)
Area: 56,345 sq mi (145,933 sq km)
State Bird: cardinal
State Tree: white oak
Statehood: 1818

The Prairie State is the official nickname of Illinois because of the native grasslands found there. It is also known as the Land of Lincoln because Abraham Lincoln spent most of his life in Illinois before going to Washington to serve as president. Ulysses S. Grant and Ronald Reagan also have connections with Illinois. Reagan was born in Tampico, and Grant lived in Galena.

Illinois is bordered to the north by Wisconsin, to the northeast by Lake Michigan, to the east and southeast by Indiana, and to the south by Kentucky. Even though the capital is Springfield, Chicago is the largest city in the state and the third largest in the U.S. Chicago is often referred to as the Windy City because of the winds blowing in from Lake Michigan. However, a popular myth states that a New York City writer gave the city its nickname because he thought the people bragged too much about their city.

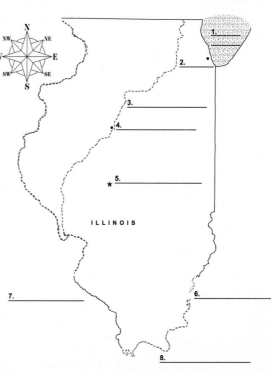

Directions: Use an atlas to label the various places numbered on the map.

Minnesota (MN)

Quick Facts

Capital: St. Paul
Population: 4,919,479 (2000 census)
Area: 86,943 sq miles (225,181 sq km)
State Bird: common loon
State Tree: red pine or Norway pine
Statehood: 1858

Minnesota's name means "water that reflects the sky" in the language of the Dakota Sioux. One of Minnesota's many nicknames is the Land of 10,000 Lakes; however, the state actually has about 12,000 lakes. At one time, Lake Itasca was thought to be the source of the Mississippi River; however, now geographers say that the real source is the streams that flow into the lake. The northernmost point in the continental United States, the Northwest Angle, is found in Minnesota. The official nickname of Minnesota, the North Star State, comes from its location.

Much of the nation's iron ore comes from Minnesota. Iron ore was discovered in the 1880s. Since that time, the mining industry has grown rapidly. Iron ore is shipped across the Great Lakes to cities in Ohio, Pennsylvania, and Indiana to produce steel.

Minneapolis, the largest city in the state, sits across the Mississippi River from its twin city, St. Paul, the capital of Minnesota. About ten miles from the Twin Cities is the city of Bloomington, where the Mall of America is located. The largest mall in the United States, it sits on seventy-eight acres. The mall includes an amusement park, a walk-through aquarium, and hundreds of shops and restaurants.

Directions: Answer the following questions.

1. The largest city in Minnesota is _____.
2. The name *Minnesota* means _____.
3. _____ has been mined in Minnesota since the 1880s.
4. Even though one of Minnesota's nicknames is the Land of 10,000 Lakes, it actually has about _____ lakes.

43

Quick Facts

Capital: Columbus
Population: 11,353,140 (2000 census)
Area: 40,952 sq miles (106,067 sq km)
State Bird: cardinal
State Tree: buckeye
Statehood: 1803

OHIO

.Columbus

Ohio comes from an Iroquois word meaning **"great river."** Ohio has three nicknames. The official nickname, **Buckeye State,** comes from the state tree. Another nickname, **Mother of Presidents**, comes from Ohio's being the birthplace of seven U.S. **presidents**. The third nickname, Mother of Invention, was earned because the state has produced such famous inventors as the **Wright Brothers**, R. E. Oldsmobile, and **Thomas Edison**.

The three largest cities are **Cleveland**, Cincinnati, and Columbus, the state capital. Cleveland, on the shore of Lake Erie, is the site of the Rock and Roll Hall of Fame. Columbus is in the center of the state. Cincinnati, on the banks of the **Ohio River**, was once known as the "Queen City of the West." **Akron** is known for its rubber manufacturing. **Canton** is the home of the Pro Football Hall of Fame.

Ohio Jumble: Locate the words shown in boldface above in the word search puzzle. The words can be found horizontally, vertically, or diagonally.

```
c n o t n a c c d y b m v u o n o a
t u d f a c l e v e l a n d p x p w
j n e j c p w p l l s l p c g w x y
s e g n b d b y l w i i u t l m r f
e v z l c b x q o f d t w v f o s r
c g x v i q h q e c n i y l v m o t
d v i h k i z c h p h j g l w f f t
p o c r v t h o m a s e d i s o n a
g g i n y s g f a k r o n s i o y w
a j z h o p s u r l l g r z a g c r
s t n e d i s e r p f o r e h t o m
u k q k v p r e s i d e n t s t s f
n p m q x g w w h t c y p f m j k h
h f b u c k e y e s t a t e x a t z
i q u q j e n u r e v i r t a e r g
o h i o r i v e r w g k t u i e x w
e t g k n y x h y o t z k l v a s e
u q s w r i g h t b r o t h e r s g
```

Quick Facts

Capital: Indianapolis
Population: 6,080,485 (2000 census)
Area: 36,185 sq miles (93,719 sq km)
State Bird: cardinal
State Tree: tulip tree or yellow poplar
Statehood: 1816

Indiana ranks among the top ten agricultural states. Its main crops are soybeans, corn, and wheat. There are thousands of farms in the state, many belonging to the Amish and Mennonites who have lived in the state since the 1800s. Almost 95 percent of the state's produce is shipped to other parts of the U.S.

Indiana is bordered by Lake Michigan and the state of Minnesota to the north. The Ohio River separates Indiana from Kentucky in the south. It is bordered to the east by Ohio.

Indianapolis, the capital and largest city, is sometimes known as the "Crossroads of America." This city has many highways which emerge from the city like the spokes on a wheel. The largest sporting event in the world, the Indianapolis 500 Auto Race, is held every year over the Memorial Day weekend. The race attracts over half a million fans each year. The Pacers, Indiana's pro basketball team, also attract many fans. South Bend is the site of the National College Football Hall of Fame.

Indiana has produced many famous "Hoosiers," including William Henry Harrison, who served as U.S. president for the shortest period of time. Astronauts Gus Grissom and Frank Borman and gangster John Dillinger are also well known Indiana natives.

Inquiring Indiana: Match the places, people, and things on the left with the descriptions on the right.

_____	1. Pacers	**A.** capital and largest city
_____	2. Indianapolis	**B.** gangster
_____	3. South Bend	**C.** astronaut
_____	4. Gus Grissom	**D.** main crop
_____	5. soybeans	**E.** pro basketball team
_____	6. John Dillinger	**F.** National College Football Hall of Fame

U.S. Geography 4–5—RB-904003

Wisconsin (WI)

Quick Facts

Capital: Madison
Population: 5,363,675 (2000 census)
Area: 54,313 sq miles (140,672 sq km)
State Bird: robin
State Tree: sugar maple
Statehood: 1848

WISCONSIN

Madison .

Wisconsin is nicknamed the Badger State because of the actions of early miners who wanted to get rich quick. These miners hurried to mine the lead found in the southwestern part of the state. Instead of taking the time to build real homes, these men dug cavelike dwellings into the hillsides. The miners were soon nicknamed "badgers."

This state remains the nation's leading dairy state, producing much of the milk, cheese, and butter for the U.S. Not surprisingly, there are almost as many cows as there are people. The largest cheese ever made, weighing 345,910 pounds and larger than three elephants, was made in Wisconsin. Besides the dairy industry, many farms produce beets, peas, cherries, corn, hay, soybeans, and cranberries.

Wisconsin has produced many famous citizens, including Frank Lloyd Wright, a famous architect, and Orson Welles, a famous actor, director, producer, and writer.

---

1. Which crop has produced the most? _____

2. Which two crops produce the least? _____ and _____

3. Are there more soybeans or hay produced? _____

4. _____ crops are shown.

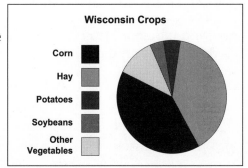

Wisconsin Crops

Corn
Hay
Potatoes
Soybeans
Other Vegetables

46

Great Lakes Madness

Directions: Match the state capital, tree, bird, and year of statehood with the correct state from the Great Lakes region.

1. Columbus
   buckeye
   cardinal
   1803

   A. Wisconsin

   B. Minnesota

2. Lansing
   white pine
   robin
   1837

   C. Michigan

3. Madison
   sugar maple
   robin
   1848

   D. Ohio

4. Indianapolis
   tulip poplar
   cardinal
   1816

   E. Illinois

5. St. Paul
   red pine
   common loon
   1858

   F. Indiana

6. Springfield
   white oak
   cardinal
   1818

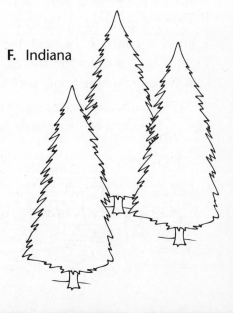

U.S. Geography 4–5—RB-904003

Southwest Region

The Southwest region is drier than the adjoining Plains region. This region, which includes New Mexico, Texas, Oklahoma, and Arizona, contains large open plains, mountains, and deserts. The magnificent Grand Canyon, formed by the Colorado River and stretching 277 miles (450 km), is located here. The Grand Canyon contains many layers of beautifully colored rock which show the development of the earth over millions of years. Visitors are constantly attracted to the majestic Grand Canyon. Its climate and vegetation are drastically different at different elevations. The floor of the canyon is similar to the Mexican desert; however, the north rim resembles southern Canada.

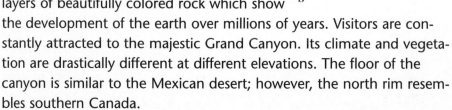

Outside of the cities, the Southwest region is full of open spaces. Much of this area is desert, though this barren American desert has been growing smaller since the end of the nineteenth century. Settlers learned that they could grow corn on the prairies and that the grassland was perfect for growing wheat or feeding cattle and sheep. As the settlers learned to cultivate the land, the size of the desert decreased. Dams built along the Colorado and other rivers have brought water to towns that were once very small, such as Las Vegas, Phoenix, and Albuquerque.

The Southwest is the largest oil producing region in the United States. The state of Texas ranks first, Oklahoma fifth, and New Mexico

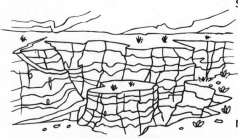

seventh in the production of oil. Much of the oil comes from the Gulf of Mexico. Sand, gypsum, cotton, cattle, uranium, wheat, copper, and hay are other resources found in the Southwest region.

Oklahoma (OK)

Quick Facts

Capital: Oklahoma City
Population: 3,450,654 (2000 census)
Area: 68,678 sq miles (177,877 sq km)
State Bird: scissor-tailed flycatcher
State Tree: redbud
Statehood: 1907

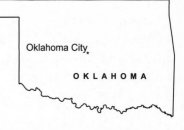

Oklahoma City

OKLAHOMA

Oklahoma is bordered by Kansas and Colorado to the north, Texas to the south, Missouri and Arkansas to the east, and New Mexico to the west. The state's outline resembles a clenched fist with a pointing finger. This finger area is known as a panhandle, and it stretches for 175 miles (282 km) to the border of New Mexico. The main landforms are flat, fertile plains and low hills. The plains here are perfect for growing wheat and for herding cattle. The Ozark Plateau and numerous valleys are located in the northeastern region of Oklahoma. The Prairie Plains, where most of the oil and coal are found, lie to the west and south in the state.

Hay and wheat are the main crops grown in the dry areas of this state. In areas where moisture is more prevalent, sorghum, peanuts, and cotton are grown. The main manufactured goods are plastics, machinery, and rubber products. Oil and cattle ranching bring in most of the income in the state. Rodeos are popular in Oklahoma's cattle country.

Directions: Circle the **best** answer for the questions below.

1. Which state borders Oklahoma to the south?
   A. Texas   **C.** New Mexico
   B. Kansas   **D.** Arkansas
2. All of the following are manufactured goods from Oklahoma except
   A. machinery.   **C.** rubber products.
   B. sorghum.   **D.** plastics.
3. Oklahoma's outline resembles
   A. fertile plains.   **C.** low hills.
   B. a clenched fist.   **D.** a finger.

U.S. Geography 4–5—RB-904003

Quick Facts

Capital: Phoenix
Population: 5,130,632 (2000 census)
Area: 113,642 sq miles (294,333 sq km)
State Bird: cactus wren
State Tree: palo verde
Statehood: 1912

The name *Arizona*, which means "place of the small spring," comes from the name of a Pima Indian village located in what is now Mexico. The state has a variety of nicknames. The most widely accepted nickname is the Grand Canyon State because of the state's most famous natural wonder. Another nickname, Baby State, was given to the state because of its late admission to the Union. Its mineral wealth is the reason for the nickname Copper State. Because of the reptile population—including coral snakes, king snakes, the Arizona mud turtle, the Gila monsters, and rattlesnakes—the state is also nicknamed "rattlesnake heaven."

A great deal of Arizona is desert land. The state has a varied climate pattern because of its wide range of elevation. The highest recorded temperature in the desert is 127°F. In some of the higher mountain elevations, temperatures often reach below zero.

Directions: Study the map and answer the following questions.

1. _____ Park is found in the SE.

2. The capital of Arizona is _____.

3. Grand Canyon National Park is in the _____ part of the state.

4. The _____ River runs across the south.

5. London Bridge is located in _____ City.

50

Texas (TX)

Quick Facts

Capital: Austin
Population: 20,851,820 (2000 census)
Area: 261,914 sq miles (678,358 sq km)
State Bird: mockingbird
State Tree: pecan
Statehood: 1845

Texas is the second largest state in population and size. The state is one of the richest because of its **oil** wealth. The site of the first great oil strike was **Spindletop**. Before the discovery of oil, **cattle** and **cotton** were the state's main products. More than thirteen million cattle a year are raised in Texas.

Four U.S. **Presidents** have called Texas their home: George W. Bush, Dwight Eisenhower, **Lyndon Johnson**, and George H. W. Bush. Sam Houston, Sandra Day O'Connor, **Dan Rather**, and George Strait are other famous people from Texas.

A variety of landscapes abound in Texas. The dry Texas **Panhandle**, which is flat as a pancake, is located between Oklahoma and New Mexico. **Big Bend** National Park, along the **Rio Grande** in the south, is so large the entire state of Rhode Island could fit inside of it.

Texas Jumble: Locate the words shown in boldface above in the word search puzzle. The words can be found horizontally, vertically, or diagonally.

s	p	e	d	n	e	b	g	i	b	t	p	s
t	e	d	i	o	m	a	d	f	o	f	p	q
n	v	n	n	s	i	f	p	m	j	y	o	z
e	h	a	c	n	r	r	a	n	x	g	t	f
d	d	r	a	h	g	e	n	l	s	m	e	r
i	l	g	t	o	q	h	h	o	l	h	l	n
s	b	o	t	j	p	t	a	b	a	p	d	q
e	f	i	l	n	n	a	n	x	c	s	n	x
r	l	r	e	o	b	r	d	o	i	e	i	r
p	o	z	t	d	x	n	l	o	m	t	p	p
l	w	u	m	n	f	a	e	d	e	x	s	h
j	i	o	d	y	v	d	n	r	h	o	i	h
o	k	o	m	l	p	c	u	v	c	d	c	e

51

New Mexico (NM)

Quick Facts

Capital: Santa Fe
Population: 1,819,046 (2000 census)
Area: 121,364 sq miles (314,334 sq km)
State Bird: roadrunner
State Tree: piñon pine
Statehood: 1912

The fifth largest U.S. state, New Mexico, is definitely the Land of Enchantment because of its beautiful landscapes. Carlsbad Caverns National Park, which encompasses one hundred caves, contains one of the largest underground caverns in the world. Geologists believe these caverns were formed between sixty and seventy million years ago. Spectacular views of deep canyons and the surrounding terrain of the Sandia Mountains can be seen in the Cibola National Forest.

Beef cattle and dairy herds are the largest agricultural industries. New Mexico is the largest producer of chili peppers in the United States. New Mexico also produces over 450 different minerals. The state has large deposits of copper and uranium along with coal, natural gas, and petroleum.

New Mexico has been influenced by the Spanish. Today, this influence can be seen in the old churches, in place names, in foods, and in customs and holidays. Several colorful people, including Billy the Kid, Geronimo, and Kit Carson, played a large part in the history of the region in territorial days.

Knowing New Mexico: Match the following places and things on the left with the descriptions on the right.

1. Carlsbad   A. minerals produced
2. Cibola National Forest   B. largest producer in the U.S.
3. chili peppers   C. capital city
4. Santa Fe   D. large underground cavern
5. over 450   E. colorful character of this region
6. Geronimo   F. location of Sandia Mountains

Complete the puzzle using the clues shown below.

Across:

1. The state tree of Oklahoma.
5. New Mexico has been influenced by the _____.
7. This part of Texas is flat as a pancake and very dry.
9. Land of _____ is New Mexico's nickname.
10. The first great oil strike in Texas was in _____.

Down:

2. Two presidents with this same last name came from Texas.
3. Most of the oil and coal in Oklahoma are found in the Prairie _____.
4. This state's outline resembles a clenched fist with a pointing finger.
6. Arizona's state tree is the _____.
8. Much of this state is desert land.

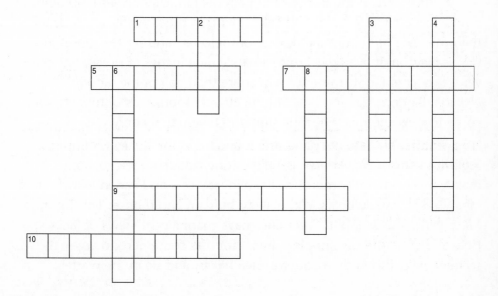

Rocky Mountain Region

The Rocky Mountain region consists of Utah, Wyoming, Idaho, Montana, Nevada, and Colorado. The greatest mountain range in North America, the Rocky Mountains, crosses through this region from north to south. Here one can also find deserts, plains, and plateaus. Much of the region is thinly populated wilderness; however, some cities in the region are among the fastest growing in the U.S.

One of the highest elevations in the United States is located in the largest city of the Rocky Mountain region: Denver, Colorado. Denver was settled in 1858 by miners and gold prospectors. This city has become the transportation, industrial, and financial leader of the region. Rocky Mountain National Park, located in Estes Park, Colorado, is the site of snow-covered peaks, waterfalls, deep forests, and meadows full of wildflowers. Another Colorado attraction is Mesa Verde National Park, home to thousands of archaeological sites.

Another state in the Rocky Mountain Region, Utah, is a mountainous, semidesert area. The Great Salt Lake, found in the Great Basin, is larger than the state of Rhode Island. One of the driest and hottest states in the U.S. is Nevada. It averages approximately nine inches of precipitation a year. The federal government owns more than half of the land in Nevada. Bighorn Canyon in Montana attracts thousands of tourists who come to view the many historic sites and beautiful scenery.

Even though national parks are abundant in the Rocky Mountain region, the most well known is Yellowstone National Park, located mainly in Wyoming. Famous for its many geysers and varied wildlife, it is inhabited by grizzly bears, elk, wolves, buffalo, and moose. The Teton Mountains, also found in Wyoming, have magnificent views of Jackson Hole as well as the surrounding areas. Tourists come here to enjoy the scenery, hike, fish in the beautiful, clear lakes, and ski in the winter.

www.summerbridgeactivities.com © Rainbow Bridge Publishing

Quick Facts

Capital: Salt Lake City
Population: 2,233,169 (2000 census)
Area: 82,168 sq miles (212,815 sq km)
State Bird: California gull
State Tree: blue spruce
Statehood: 1896

Approximately 140 million years ago, the land that is eastern Utah contained a major river. During the Jurassic Period, dinosaurs lived and died near this river. In 1909, Earl Douglass, a scientist, discovered thousands of dinosaur bones in this area. This was the largest concentration of dinosaur bones in the world. Today, these bones can be seen by visitors at the Dinosaur National Monument in Vernal, Utah.

The Great Salt Lake, covering over 1,700 miles, is the largest lake west of the Mississippi River. It is seven times saltier than the oceans. Utah has a variety of interestingly shaped geographic features. Arches National Park has pinnacles, towers, and almost perfect arches shaped by wind and weather. Bryce Canyon National Park has rock spires that appear to grow up from the canyon floor. Zion Canyon, in Zion National Park, is so deep that sunlight rarely makes it to the bottom.

The state capital, Salt Lake City, is the location of the world center of The Church of Jesus Christ of Latter-day Saints (Mormons). The church's temple, located in downtown Salt Lake City, is a six-spired building that took forty years to complete. The first Mormons came to Utah in 1847 led by Brigham Young, who became governor in 1850.

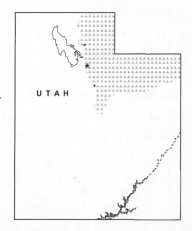

Mapping Utah: Using an atlas of the U.S., locate and label the following on the map: Salt Lake City, Ogden, Provo, Colorado River, The Great Salt Lake, and the Rocky Mountains.

U.S. Geography 4–5—RB-904003

Wyoming (WY)

Quick Facts

Capital: Cheyenne
Population: 493,782 (2000 census)
Area: 97,104 sq miles (251,500 sq km)
State Bird: western meadowlark
State Tree: cottonwood
Statehood: 1890

WYOMING

Cheyenne *

Wyoming, famous for its beautiful mountains, is the setting for the world's oldest national park, Yellowstone. The park contains the famous geyser Old Faithful which erupts every 30 to 90 minutes, sending 5,000 to 8,000 gallons of steam and spray into the air. Bison, elk, antelope, deer, gray wolves, and bears can be found in the park. Grand Teton National Park and Jackson Hole are located not far from Yellowstone. The first national monument in the U.S., Devil's Tower, is a giant stump-shaped rock that rises 1,267 feet above the plains.

There are many "firsts" for the state of Wyoming. Wyoming was the first state to allow women to vote, the first to elect a female governor, and the first to appoint a female justice of the peace.

Ranching is an important part of Wyoming's economy. About one half of the state's land is used for grazing. Thousands of oil wells can be found on the state's prairies. Wyoming is an important mining state because of its petroleum, coal, and natural gas. The main agricultural products include hay, wheat, barley, sugar, and corn.

Directions: Answer the following questions.

1. The world's oldest national park is _____.

2. _____ is an important part of Wyoming's economy.

3. The capital city of Wyoming is _____.

4. _____ was the first national monument in the United States.

5. The famous geyser _____ is found in Yellowstone.

6. Jackson Hole and _____ National Park are located not far from Yellowstone.

Quick Facts

Capital: Helena
Population: 902,195 (2000 census)
Area: 145,556 sq miles (376,990 sq km)
State Bird: western meadowlark
State Tree: ponderosa pine
Statehood: 1889

MONTANA

Helena

Early visitors saw the sun glistening on the snowcapped **mountains** and nicknamed Montana "the land of the shining mountains." These mountains held **silver** and **gold**, which is why Montana's official nickname is the **Treasure State**. Montana also contains broad plains in the east. The view from these large open plains gives this state another nickname, **Big Sky Country**.

Montana is bordered to the east by North and South Dakota, to the west by Idaho, to the south by Idaho and Wyoming, and to the north by Canada. It is the fourth largest state in size. The three main rivers found in the state are the **Missouri**, **Yellowstone**, and **Marias**.

Tourism plays an important part in the economy of Montana. Montana is home to the northern portion of Yellowstone National Park, **Glacier** National Park, Little Big Horn National Monument, the Big Horn Canyon National Recreation Area, and several other national monuments.

Montana Jumble: Locate the words shown in boldface above in the word search puzzle. The words can be found horizontally or vertically.

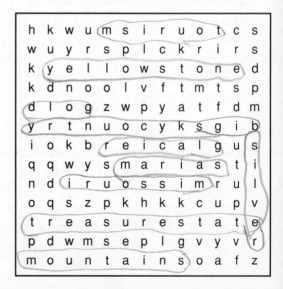

h	k	w	u	m	s	i	r	u	o	t	c	s
w	u	y	r	s	p	l	c	k	r	i	r	s
k	y	e	l	l	o	w	s	t	o	n	e	d
k	d	n	o	o	l	v	f	t	m	t	s	p
d	l	o	g	z	w	p	y	a	t	f	d	m
y	r	t	n	u	o	c	y	k	s	g	i	b
i	o	k	b	r	e	i	c	a	l	g	u	s
q	q	w	y	s	m	a	r	i	a	s	t	i
n	d	i	r	u	o	s	s	i	m	r	u	l
o	q	s	z	p	k	h	k	k	c	u	p	v
t	r	e	a	s	u	r	e	s	t	a	t	e
p	d	w	m	s	e	p	l	g	v	y	v	r
m	o	u	n	t	a	i	n	s	o	a	f	z

Quick Facts

Capital: Boise
Population: 1,293,953 (2000 census)
Area: 82,751 sq miles (214,325 sq km)
State Bird: mountain bluebird
State Tree: western white pine
Statehood: 1890

    With more wilderness than any other state, Idaho is dominated by exciting scenery, towering snow-capped mountains, enormous natural resources, peaceful lakes, steep canyons, and large forests. Idaho's wilderness areas lure many hikers, skiers, white-water rafters, and numerous other nature lovers. The untamed landscape has earned Idaho the reputation as the wildest state. It is no wonder with place names such as Snake River, Sawtooth Mountains, Lava Hot Springs, River of No Return, and Hell's Canyon.

    There were major discoveries of silver in the 1880s and gold in the 1860s in Idaho. Other gems found in the state include sapphires, rubies, diamonds, opals, and topaz. Star garnets have been found near the lake known as Coeur d'Alene.

    Another nickname for Idaho is the "spud state" because of its potato production. Farmers here grow more potatoes than any other state. More than 25 percent of potatoes grown in this country come from Idaho. The main region for potato growing is in the lower, wider part of the state, which is irrigated by the Snake River. Visitors to the Idaho Potato Expo in Blackfoot can see the world's largest potato chip, which measures two feet by fourteen inches.

Come to Idaho Travel Poster Directions: On a separate sheet of paper, create a travel poster to entice tourists to visit Idaho. Across the top of the page, print IDAHO in large, bold, colorful letters. At the bottom of the page, choose two or three words that would best describe the state. In the center of the poster, draw a picture of a symbol or a particular site that you feel best represents this state. Make your picture neat and colorful.

Nevada (NV)

Quick Facts

Capital: Carson City
Population: 1,998,257 (2000 census)
Area: 109,805 sq miles (284,396 sq km)
State Bird: mountain bluebird
State Tree: bristlecone pine
Statehood: 1864

The state of Nevada was originally part of Mexico. Its name is Spanish for "snow-covered" and refers to the Sierra Nevada mountain range found on the western border of the state. Because these mountains are so tall, they block clouds from the West, causing Nevada to be a desert with extremely high temperatures. The average high temperature in July in Las Vegas, Nevada is 105°F.

Las Vegas, the state's largest city, is the main tourist attraction with its large and luxurious hotels and gambling casinos. Another attraction is Hoover Dam. Work on the dam, which was built on the Colorado River, began in 1931 and continued for five years. A major engineering and construction feat in its time, Hoover Dam was once the largest dam in the world. More than six million tons of concrete were used to complete the dam, which is more than 726 feet tall.

Carson City, the capital, is named for Kit Carson, an Indian fighter. Though silver changed Virginia City into a bustling town, this city is now a ghost town with 1.5 million visitors each year. Lake Tahoe, a ski resort near Reno, is found on the border of California.

The state's most valuable field crop is hay, which is primarily grown in the northwest. Ranches and farms cover about an eighth of the state.

Knowing Nevada: Match the places and things on the left with the descriptions on the right.

1. Virginia City
2. Sierra Nevada
3. Kit Carson
4. Nevada
5. hay
6. Hoover Dam

A. more than 726 feet tall
B. means "snow-covered"
C. Indian fighter
D. most valuable crop
E. ghost town
F. mountain range

U.S. Geography 4–5—RB-904003

Quick Facts

Capital: Denver
Population: 4,301,261 (2000 census)
Area: 103,728 sq miles (268,657 sq km)
State Bird: lark bunting
State Tree: blue spruce
Statehood: 1876

Denver

COLORADO

Colorado is bordered by Wyoming to the north, Nebraska and Kansas to the east, Oklahoma, New Mexico, and Arizona to the south, and Utah to the west. This state has the highest average altitude of any state in the U.S. The Rocky Mountains, the Rio Grande, and the Colorado River help make this one of the most beautiful states. The highest peak of the Rocky Mountains, Mount Elbert, is located in Colorado. The eastern part of the state is part of the Great Plains. Denver, the capital city, is found in the eastern part of the state and has an elevation of one mile.

Tourism is an important part of Colorado's economy. Colorado Springs became a popular health spa in the 1860s. Today, it is the location of the U.S. Air Force Academy. Aspen and Vail are two of the most popular ski resorts in the U.S. Mesa Verde National Park, Dinosaur National Monument, and Rocky Mountain National Park are also popular tourist attractions. Pikes Peak, located north of Denver, was named for Zebulon Pike. In 1893, Katherine Lee Bates wrote the song "America the Beautiful" while visiting Pikes Peak.

Directions: Study this map and a regional map and answer the following questions.

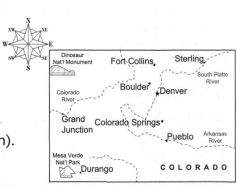

1. The city of Pueblo is located along the _____ River.

2. Dinosaur National Monument is in the _____ (direction).

3. What two states border Colorado to the east?
   _____ and _____

Rocky Mountain Farm Graph

Directions: Study the graph below to answer the questions.

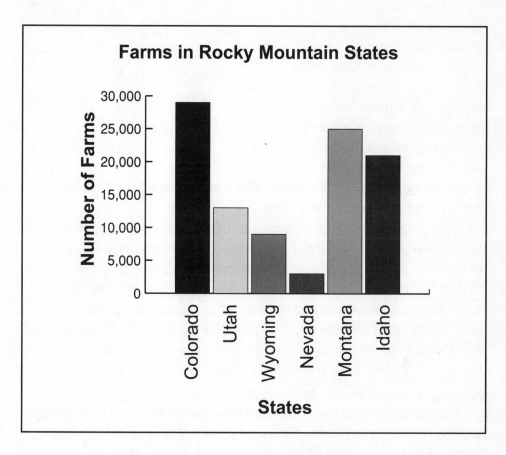

Farms in Rocky Mountain States

1. _____ has the largest number of farms.

2. Both _____ and _____ have fewer farms than Utah.

3. Montana has about _____ farms.

4. Colorado has _____ more farms than Montana.

5. There are ____ states represented on this graph.

6. Wyoming has about _____ less farms than Colorado.

7. Nevada, Wyoming, and Utah have about _____ farms.

© Rainbow Bridge Publishing   U.S. Geography 4–5—RB-904003

The Pacific region consists of Hawaii, Washington, California, Alaska, and Oregon. The Pacific Coast states have dense forests, spectacular ocean shores, and rugged mountains. The climate in most of this region is generally mild with moderate to extreme precipitation depending on the closeness to the ocean. There are some areas inland which are dry with temperature extremes.

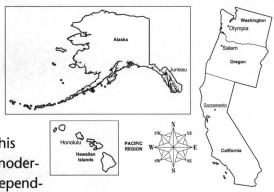

The large geographical distances in the Pacific region give it the largest geographical variety of any region. From the islands of Hawaii, which are made of volcanoes, to Alaska's frozen tundra, the region varies in both landforms and climate. Washington, Oregon, and California have dramatic landscapes provided by valleys, mountains, and coastlines. Northeastern Washington contains the northern Rocky Mountains. The Cascade Range becomes the Sierra Nevada Range when it reaches California. Another long line of mountains are the Coast Ranges which extend from southeastern Alaska to southern California.

Oil and timber are some of the natural resources found in this rich region. Oregon and Washington supply more timber than any other region. The fertile valleys of California provide perfect land for growing fruits and vegetables. The main businesses of the region include mining, lumbering, manufacturing, truck farming, and the citrus and wine industries.

Besides the geographical differences, this region contains a vast ethnic diversity. Along with the native Hawaiians and Inuit, there are also many Asians, Hispanics, African Americans, and Caucasians. Population continues to be more condensed in California than farther north. The main cities in the region include Los Angeles, San Diego, San Francisco, Seattle, Portland, Honolulu, and Anchorage.

Hawaii (HI)

Quick Facts

Honolulu ★

H A W A I I A N
I S L A N D S

Capital: Honolulu
Population: 1,211,537 (2000 census)
Area: 6,423 sq miles (16,636 sq km)
State Bird: nene (Hawaiian goose)
State Tree: kukui (candlenut)
Statehood: 1959

Hawaii includes 132 islets. The eight major islands are Hawaii, **Oahu**, **Maui**, Molokai, Kahoolawe, Kauai, Lanai, and Niihau. These volcanic islands were formed long ago when a rift opened in the bottom of the Pacific Ocean and lava emerged. The largest island, **Hawaii**, is home to two active **volcanoes**, **Mauna Loa** and **Kilauea**, part of Hawaii Volcanoes National Park. Black sand beaches, waterfalls, rain forests, and exotic reefs make Hawaii a virtual paradise.

Tourism is the major industry of Hawaii. The *USS Arizona* Memorial at **Pearl Harbor**, Hulihee and Iolani Palaces, and the Waikiki resort area are main attractions. **Sugar** and **pineapple** are Hawaii's main exports.

Hawaii is known as the Aloha State. In the native language, *aloha*, which means "love," is both a greeting and a farewell.

Hawaii Jumble: Locate the words shown in boldface above in the word search puzzle. The words can be found horizontally, vertically, or diagonally.

s	b	t	i	i	a	w	a	h	l	f
k	h	n	r	j	q	o	o	y	r	z
p	e	a	r	l	h	a	r	b	o	r
i	j	z	f	w	u	y	p	q	s	j
s	e	o	n	a	c	l	o	v	u	a
k	i	l	a	u	e	a	u	n	g	v
w	a	n	a	a	c	h	h	v	a	m
j	h	r	i	u	a	m	t	m	r	v
b	o	g	w	o	v	b	z	l	v	h
x	l	p	i	n	e	a	p	p	l	e
n	a	a	o	l	a	n	u	a	m	i

U.S. Geography 4–5—RB-904003

Quick Facts

Capital: Olympia
Population: 5,894,121 (2000 census)
Area: 66,581 sq miles (172,445 sq km)
State Bird: willow goldfinch
State Tree: western hemlock
Statehood: 1889

Washington, the only state named after a president, is bordered to the west by the Pacific Ocean, to the south by Oregon, to the east by Idaho, and to the north by Canada. The location of this state makes it a gateway for land, sea, and air travel to Alaska and countries across the Pacific.

Mount Rainier, the highest mountain in the state, is a dormant volcano. Climbers ascend this mountain to prepare for climbing Mt. Everest. Mount St. Helens is an active volcanic mountain located in Washington. Both of these mountains are part of the Cascade Mountain Range.

The nation's largest producer of hydroelectric power, the Grand Coulee Dam, was completed in 1942. This dam is also used in farm irrigation. The production of aluminum, one of the state's main industries, requires large amounts of electricity. Most of the needed power comes from hydroelectric dams.

More than two-thirds of the state is covered with national forests and parklands. The lumber and paper industries have been important to the state's economy for a long time.

Directions: Answer the following questions.

1. The highest mountain in the state is _____.

2. Washington is bordered by the _____ to the west.

3. More than _____ of the state is covered with forests.

4. The _____ is the largest producer of hydroelectric power in the U.S.

5. The state bird of Washington is the _____.

6. _____ is an active volcanic mountain.

California (CA)

Quick Facts

Capital: Sacramento
Population: 33,871,648 (2000 census)
Area: 155,973 sq miles (403,970 sq km)
State Bird: California valley quail
State Tree: redwood
Statehood: 1850

California contains many types of geographical features. The Central Valley, a huge fertile valley, is bordered by the Coast Range to the west and the Sierra Nevada to the east. This valley is naturally irrigated by mountain-fed rivers. The highest peak in the continental U.S., Mount Whitney, is located in the Sierra Nevada. These mountains are also the location of the world famous Yosemite National Park. The Mojave Desert is in the south central part of the state. North and east of this desert is Death Valley, which contains the hottest and lowest point in North America.

The main industry in California is agriculture, including the production of fruits, vegetables, and wine. Aerospace, entertainment, and light manufacturing, including computer hardware and software, are also important to the state. Tourism is another important factor in the economy. Disneyland, Sea World, Yosemite Falls, and Hollywood are just some of the numerous attractions.

There are many famous people from California, including Joe DiMaggio, John Steinbeck, Ronald Reagan, Richard Nixon, Robert Frost, and Tiger Woods. Herbert Hoover, former U.S. president, lived much of his life in the state.

Colorful California: Match the places, people, and things on the left with the descriptions on the right.

1. Herbert Hoover
2. Disneyland
3. Mount Whitney
4. agriculture
5. Death Valley
6. Tiger Woods
7. Mojave Desert

A. highest peak in continental U.S.
B. found in south central California
C. famous California attraction
D. hottest and lowest point in U.S.
E. former U.S. President
F. main industry
G. famous Californian

65

Alaska (AK)

Quick Facts

Capital: Juneau
Population: 626,932 (2000 census)
Area: 570,374 sq miles (1,477,267 sq km)
State Bird: willow ptarmigan
State Tree: Sitka spruce
Statehood: 1959

Alaska is our largest state in area; however, it has one of the smallest populations. The name *Alaska* comes from an Aleutian word, *alakshak*, which means "great land." The state was nicknamed the Last Frontier because it is the least explored and settled state in the United States. Alaska is one of two states in North America that is not a part of the forty-eight contiguous states.

Alaska has several geographical regions. South central Alaska includes the southern coastal region with many towns, cities, and industrial sites. The Alaska Panhandle in the southeast is home to numerous glaciers and forests. In the interior of Alaska, there are large rivers, such as the Yukon and the Kuskokwim, along with the tundra. The Aleutian Islands extend west from the southern tip of Alaska and include many active volcanoes. Mount McKinley, the highest peak in North America, is found in Denali National Park and Preserve, north of Anchorage.

Alaska is often called the Land of the Midnight Sun. In Barrow, located on the northern border, the sun shines constantly for eighty-four days from May 10 to August 2. There is no sunshine in Barrow for sixty-seven days from November 18 to January 24. The state receives a large amount of snow. Some parts of the state average twenty feet per year.

Plan an Alaskan Vacation
Directions: Use a map to plan a seven-day vacation to Alaska. Include stops in at least two national parks and at least three cities. Describe some of the sights that you will see.

66

Quick Facts

Capital: Salem
Population: 3,421,399 (2000 census)
Area: 96,002 sq miles (248,646 sq km)
State Bird: western meadowlark
State Tree: Douglas fir
Statehood: 1859

Oregon is bordered by California to the south, Idaho to the east, Washington to the north, and the Pacific Ocean to the west. Most people live inland in the fertile Willamette Valley rather than along the coastline. The coastline is open to everyone because it is public land.

The Cascade Mountain Range, which contains the large Willamette and Fremont National Forests, runs north to south through Oregon. The area west of the mountains receives large amounts of rainfall. The region east of the mountains is in a rain shadow, making eastern Oregon much drier.

Lumbering is the most important industry in the state. Oregon is the main timber-producing state in the U.S. Most of the forests are found in the Cascade and Coast Mountain Ranges. Food processing and the production of scientific instruments are also important industries. Fishing is the main industry in the western part of the state. Here both wild and farmed trout and salmon are found. Flower growing is another important economic activity found mainly in the Willamette Valley.

Overview of Oregon: Choose the best answer.

1. The most important industry in Oregon is
   A. fishing.   **C.** flowers.
   B. lumbering.   **D.** food processing.

2. The Willamette and Fremont National Forests are found in
   A. California.   **C.** Coast Mountains.
   B. Idaho.   **D.** Cascade Mountains.

3. Most people in Oregon live
   A. inland.   **C.** on the coast.
   B. in the mountains. **D.** on trout farms.

U.S. Geography 4–5—RB-904003

Pacific Timeline

Directions: Study the timeline to answer the questions.

1. When did Oregon
   become a state?

   _____

2. Did Washington become a
   territory before or after Hawaii?

   _____

3. Which state became a
   U.S. state in 1850?

   _____

4. How many years before Alaska
   was purchased did Oregon
   become a state?

   _____

5. Which two states received
   statehood in 1959?

   _____,

   _____

6. How many years
   does this timeline cover?

   _____

7. How many years had Oregon
   been a state before Alaska
   became a state? _____

8. How many Pacific states are
   represented in the timeline?

   _____.

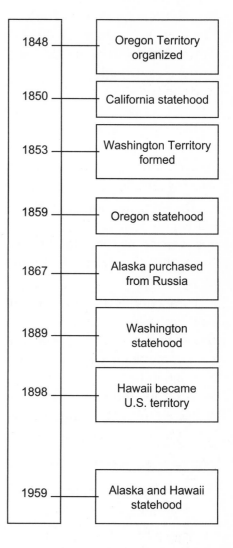

1848	Oregon Territory organized
1850	California statehood
1853	Washington Territory formed
1859	Oregon statehood
1867	Alaska purchased from Russia
1889	Washington statehood
1898	Hawaii became U.S. territory
1959	Alaska and Hawaii statehood

www.summerbridgeactivities.com
© Rainbow Bridge Publishing

U. S. Analogies

Directions: Use the information found in this book or any other resource to solve the following analogies.

1. Atlanta : Georgia :: Austin : _____

2. Chesapeake Bay : Maryland :: San Francisco Bay : _____

3. Bluegrass State : Kentucky :: Prairie State : _____

4. Old Faithful : Wyoming :: Mount Rainier : _____

5. Mojave Desert : California :: Tularosa Basin : _____

6. Providence : Rhode Island :: Juneau : _____

7. Cape Hatteras : North Carolina :: Cape Cod : _____

8. Lake Ontario : New York :: Lake Superior : _____

9. Mount Katahdin : Maine :: Magazine Mountain : _____

10. Buckeye State : Ohio :: Show Me State : _____

11. Gila River : Arizona :: Hudson River : _____

12. New Hampshire : Maine :: Alabama : _____

13. Kansas : Great Plains :: Iowa : _____

© Rainbow Bridge Publishing   U.S. Geography 4–5—RB-904003

Where Am I?

Directions: Use the clues to help you find the name of the mystery state. Write its name on the line below.

1. I am south of Oklahoma. I am west of Louisiana. The Rio Grande forms my southern border. I am one of the richest states because of my oil wealth. I am...

   _____

2. My tallest mountain is Mount Katahdin. Thousands of hikers travel over 2,000 miles from Georgia across the Appalachian Trail to me. My capital is Augusta. I am...

   _____

3. The Platte River runs across me. The Missouri River forms my eastern border. My state tree is the cottonwood. My nickname, Cornhusker State, comes from my main crop. I am...

   _____

4. Sugar and pineapple are my main exports. I am made of 132 islets. My state bird is the Nene. Kilauea is a volcano found on my main island. I am...

   _____

5. The chocolate capital of the nation, Hershey, is found in my state. I am known as the Keystone State. Harrisburg is my capital city. New York is to my north. I am...

   _____

6. Herbert Hoover was born in my state. Ninety percent of my state is farmland. The World Pork Expo is held in my capital city of Des Moines. I am...

   _____

7. Kennedy Space Center and Cape Canaveral are on my east coast. Busch Gardens is found in my city of Tampa. The country of Cuba is south of my state. Disney World is in Orlando. I am...

   _____

8. I am made of two peninsulas. I am bordered by four of the five Great Lakes. My largest city, Detroit, is often called "Motor City." Motown Records started here. I am...

   _____

U. S. Time Zones

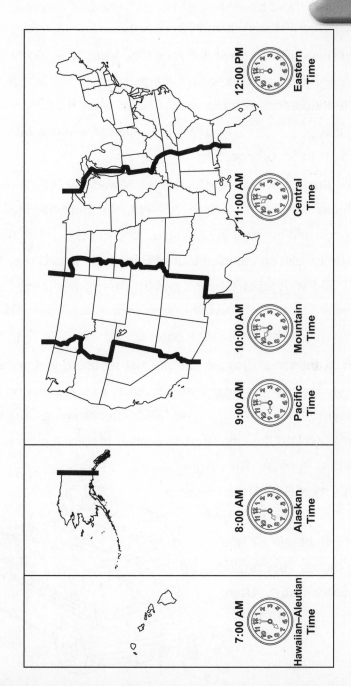

© Rainbow Bridge Publishing   U.S. Geography 4–5—RB-904003

See the USA

Directions: Travel across the USA with Grayson and Denise. Complete the story by filling in the correct time and by circling AM or PM. Use the time zone map on the previous page.

Grayson and Denise leave Salt Lake City, Utah, at 9:30 AM on Friday and drive with their parents to St. George, Utah. In St. George, they pick up their grandparents. The trip to St. George takes 6 hours; therefore, they arrive at __ __ : __ __ AM/PM. They spend the night with their grandparents in St. George.

On Saturday, they leave for Las Vegas, Nevada, at 9:20 AM. They arrive 2 hours later at __ __ : __ __ AM/PM. The family decides to spend the afternoon and evening in Las Vegas. After checking in at the hotel, they decide to take an escorted tour of Hoover Dam, and they leave the hotel at 1:00 PM. It takes 1 hour travel time to Hoover Dam. The tour bus arrives at __ __ : __ __ AM/PM. After their 2-hour tour and 1-hour return trip, they arrive back at the hotel at __ __ : __ __ AM/PM.

The next morning, Grayson and his mother board a plane and leave at 6:55 AM. The flight to New York City takes 3 hours, arriving at Kennedy Airport at __ __ : __ __ AM/PM. After claiming their luggage, they take a taxi into the city. Grayson and his mother remain in New York City until Tuesday. Their flight leaves New York City at 3:00 PM to return to Salt Lake City where their family lives. Their flight takes 2 hours and 45 minutes. They finally arrive in Salt Lake City, Utah, at __ __ : __ __ AM/PM.

Identify the States

Directions: Identify the states that border the states shown below.

1.

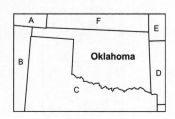

A. _____

B. _____

C. _____

D. _____

E. _____

F. _____

2.

A. _____

B. _____

C. _____

D. _____

E. _____

3.

A. _____

B. _____

C. _____

D. _____

E. _____

F. _____

4.

A. _____

B. _____

C. _____

D. _____

E. _____

Identify the States

Directions: Identify the states that border the states shown below.

5.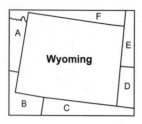

A. _____

B. _____

C. _____

D. _____

E. _____

F. _____

6.

A. _____

B. _____

C. _____

D. _____

E. _____

F. _____

7.

A. _____

B. _____

C. _____

D. _____

E. _____

8.

A. _____

B. _____

C. _____

D. _____

E. _____

F. _____

Match the Capitals

Directions: Match each state with its capital.

1. Alaska		A.	Baton Rouge
2. Arizona		B.	Santa Fe
3. Colorado		C.	Richmond
4. Connecticut		D.	Olympia
5. Florida		E.	Juneau
6. Hawaii		F.	Tallahassee
7. Idaho		G.	Columbus
8. Indiana		H.	Honolulu
9. Louisiana		I.	Madison
10. Minnesota		J.	Lincoln
11. Mississippi		K.	Montpelier
12. Montana		L.	Phoenix
13. Nebraska		M.	Indianapolis
14. Nevada		N.	Salem
15. New Mexico		O.	Boise
16. New York		P.	Cheyenne
17. North Dakota		Q.	Harrisburg
18. Ohio		R.	Denver
19. Oregon		S.	Salt Lake City
20. Pennsylvania		T.	Albany
21. Rhode Island		U.	Columbia
22. South Carolina		V.	Hartford
23. Tennessee		W.	Jackson
24. Texas		X.	Carson City
25. Utah		Y.	Providence
26. Vermont		Z.	Austin
27. Virginia		AA.	St. Paul
28. Washington		BB.	Helena
29. Wisconsin		CC.	Nashville
30. Wyoming		DD.	Bismarck

U.S. Geography 4–5—RB-904003

Page 4
1. northeastern
2. California
3. Acadia National Park
4. Glaciers
5. 30,864

Page 6
1. b
2. d
3. a
4. c

Page 8
1. Waterbury
2. maple syrup
3. tallest
4. 608,827

Page 10
1. Appalachian
2. Green
3. Canada
4. New Hampshire
5. northeastern
6. Rhode Island
7. south
8. Taconic

Page 12
Answers may vary.
1. This is where Francis Scott Key wrote "The Star Spangled Banner."
2. It is the baseball field where the Baltimore Orioles play.
3. The aquarium houses 10,000 marine specimens.
4. Ocean City is a popular resort town on a 10-mile barrier island.

Page 13

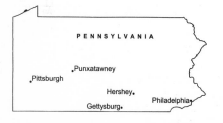

Page 14

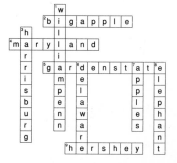

Page 15
1. Empire State Building
2. Buffalo
3. Big Apple
4. Niagara Falls
5. Adirondack Mountains
6. publishing

Page 16
1. d
2. b
3. a
4. f
5. c
6. e

Page 17

Page 19
The meaning of the state seal of Georgia is the date of signing the Declaration of Independence plus a swordsman between pillars to symbolize military aid to defend the Constitution. Adopted 1914.

Answer Pages

Page 20
1. Sassafras
2. fortieth
3. southeast
4. Hilton Head Island and Myrtle Beach

Page 21
1. e
2. a
3. b
4. d
5. c

Page 22
1. Tallahassee
2. Orlando
3. Miami
4. Tampa
5. Cape Canaveral
6. St. Augustine
7. Daytona

Page 23
1. c
2. e
3. a
4. d
5. b

Page 24

1609	1726	1727	1742	1770	1782	1796	1859	1861	1863
James I gave region to settlers	territory settled	Shepherds-town	George Washington surveyed land	Cherokee and Iroquois gave up claims to the land	battle at Wheeling	Harper's Ferry became a U.S. arsenal	John Brown seized arsenal	West Virginia separated from Virginia	West Virginia became a state

Page 25
1. b
2. c
3. b

Page 27
1. Great Smoky Mountains
2. climate and plentiful rainfall
3. Graceland
4. North Carolina

Page 28
1. Kentucky Derby
2. Louisville
3. automobile
4. prize fighter
5. Abraham Lincoln
6. Casey Jones
7. Diane Sawyer

Bluegrass State

Page 29
1. b
2. d
3. c

Page 30

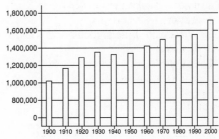

Page 31
1. d
2. g
3. i
4. l
5. a
6. k
7. f
8. j
9. e
10. c
11. h
12. b

Page 33

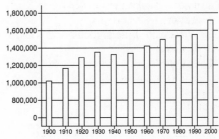

Page 34
1. 90
2. World Pork Expo
3. Herbert Hoover
4. eastern goldfinch
5. alfalfa
6. Hawkeye
7. Des Moines

© Rainbow Bridge Publishing

U.S. Geography 4–5—RB-904003

Page 36
1. c
2. e
3. g
4. b
5. f
6. a
7. h
8. d

Page 37

```
a g t f a r c r i a i y z k c
n b w e x e s b v b q g x f f
j a t y o u z e u e n l m a p
t e k s a b d a e r b w h j d
n g x f q t x p b v r u s i o
q r g m d f t s s a z s o u g
r e t a t s r e w o l f n u s
v g z w g p k z a n w j s i v
f n o s b g z b u r w p x j w
q p u w i c h i t a p h n x h
x j r k v q p i c s w i e q j
t r a h r a e a i l e m a a s
h c q v f i x t s e w d l o t
y v s i r r i g a t i o n s w
y t i c e g d o d u i v p a o
```

Page 38
1. b
2. d
3. c

Page 39
1. b
2. a
3. d
4. c
5. b
6. c

Page 41
1. Upper
2. Wisconsin, Illinois, Indiana, or Ohio
3. Grand
4. southwest

Page 42

Page 43
1. Minneapolis
2. water that reflects the sky
3. iron ore
4. 12,000

Page 44

```
c n o t n a c c d y b m v u o n o a
t u d f a c l e v e l a n d p x p w
j n e j c p w p l l s l p c g w x y
s e g n b d b y l w i i u t l m r f
e v z l c b x q o f d t w v f o s r
c g x v i q h q e c n i y l v m o t
d v i h k i z c h p h j g l w f f t
p o c r v t h o m a s e d i s o n a
g g i n y s g f a k r o n s i o y w
a j z h o p s u r l l g r z a g c r
s t n e d i s e r p f o r e h t o m
u k q k v p r e s i d e n t s t s f
n p m q x g w w h t c y p f m j k h
h f b u c k e y e s t a t e x a t z
i q u q j e n u r e v i r t a e r g
o h i o r i v e r w g k t u i e x w
e t g k n y x h y o t z k l v a s e
u q s w r i g h t b r o t h e r s g
```

Page 45
1. e
2. a
3. f
4. c
5. d
6. b

Page 46
1. corn
2. soybeans and potatoes
3. hay
4. five

Page 47
1. d
2. c
3. a
4. f
5. b
6. e

Page 49
1. a
2. b
3. b

Page 50
1. Saguaro National
2. Phoenix
3. northwest
4. Gila
5. Lake Havasu

Answer Pages

Page 51

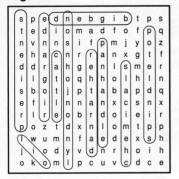

Page 52

1. d
2. f
3. b
4. c
5. a
6. e

Page 53

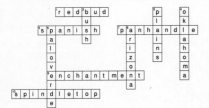

Page 55

Page 56

1. Yellowstone
2. Ranching
3. Cheyenne
4. Devil's Tower
5. Old Faithful
6. Grand Teton

Page 57

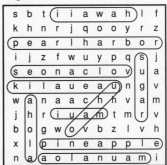

Page 59

1. e
2. f
3. c
4. b
5. d
6. a

Page 60

1. Arkansas
2. northwest
3. Kansas and Nebraska

Page 61

1. Colorado
2. Wyoming and Nevada
3. 25,000
4. 4,000
5. six
6. 20,000
7. 32,8000

Page 63

© Rainbow Bridge Publishing   U.S. Geography 4–5—RB-904003

Page 64
1. Mount Rainier
2. Pacific Ocean
3. 2/3
4. Grand Coulee Dam
5. willow goldfinch
6. Mount St. Helens

Page 65
1. e   2. c
3. a   4. f
5. d   6. g
7. b

Page 67
1. b
2. d
3. a

Page 68
1. 1859   2. before
3. California   4. eight
5. Alaska & Hawaii   6. 111
7. ten   8. five

Page 69
1. Texas   2. California
3. Kansas   4. Washington
5. New Mexico   6. Alaska
7. Massachusetts   8. Michigan
9. Arkansas   10. Missouri
11. New York   12. Georgia
13. Central Plains

Page 70
1. Texas   2. Maine
3. Nebraska   4. Hawaii
5. Pennsylvania   6. Iowa
7. Florida   8. Michigan

Page 72
1. 3:30 PM   2. 10:20 AM
3. 2:00 PM   4. 5:00 PM
5. 12:55 PM   6. 3:45 PM

Page 73
1. A. Colorado   2. A. Ohio
   B. New Mexico   B. Kentucky
   C. Texas   C. Virginia
   D. Arkansas   D. Maryland
   E. Missouri   E. Pennsylvania
   F. Kansas

3. A. Idaho   4. A. Iowa
   B. Nevada   B. Missouri
   C. Arizona   C. Kentucky
   D. New Mexico   D. Indiana
   E. Colorado   E. Wisconsin
   F. Wyoming

Page 74
5. A. Idaho   6. A. Alabama
   B. Utah   B. Florida
   C. Colorado   C. South Carolina
   D. Nebraska   D. North Carolina
   E. South Dakota   E. Tennessee
   F. Montana

7. A. California   8. A. Montana
   B. Arizona   B. Wyoming
   C. Utah   C. Nebraska
   D. Idaho   D. Iowa
   E. Oregon   E. Minnesota
   F. North Dakota

Page 75
1. E   2. L
3. R   4. V
5. F   6. H
7. O   8. M
9. A   10. AA
11. W   12. BB
13. J   14. X
15. B   16. T
17. DD   18. G
19. N   20. Q
21. Y   22. U
23. CC   24. Z
25. S   26. K
27. C   28. D
29. I   30. P